Trade Unions

Eric Wainwright

Batsford Academic and Educational Ltd
London

CONTENTS

Typeset by Tek-Art Ltd, West Wickham, Kent
and printed in Great Britain by
R.J. Acford
Chichester, Sussex
for the publishers
Batsford Academic and Educational Ltd,
an imprint of B.T. Batsford Ltd,
4 Fitzhardinge Street
London W1H 0AH

ISBN 0 7134 3570 4

ACKNOWLEDGMENTS
The Author and Publishers thank the following for
their kind permission to reproduce copyright
illustrations: BBC Hulton Picture Library, pages 6,
14, 15, 16, 17 (top), 58, 62; Central Press Photos,
page 22; Henry Grant, pages 11 (left), 46, 47; Sally
and Richard Greenhill, pages 30, 31, 54, 64; Imperial
War Museum, page 17 (bottom); Keystone Press
Agency Ltd, page 18, 33 (right), 45, 48; NUJ, page
34; Topham Picture Library, pages 11 (right), 19, 24
(left), 25, 26, 27, 33 (left), 37, 38, 39, 40, 41, 42, 50,
61, 63; TUC Library, pages 7 (G . Cossey), 10
(Central Office of Information), 12 (G. Cossey), 20,
24 (right); USDAW, page 35. The pictures were
researched by Pat Hodgson.

INTRODUCTION

You can't get me,
I'm part of the union,
Till the day I die,
Till the day I die.
(from "Part of the Union" by the STRAWBS)

Hardly a day goes past without trade unions figuring prominently in the news, in newspapers, on television and on radio. Almost everyone seems to hold very strong views about trade unions. Many believe that the unions are responsible for all, or almost all, the economic difficulties of the country. The unions are believed by some people to have far too much power and to behave in a high-handed and irresponsible way.

The pop song quoted above expresses this commonly-held view. The trade unionist is said to see himself as above the law, because of the security he gets from belonging to a union. He is bloody-minded and unco-operative. The last thing he thinks about is the success of the firm for which he is working. Rather, he prides himself on trying to make things as difficult as possible for his employers:

And I'll do what I can,
To ruin the company plan.

If he has the slightest grievance against management, the song says, he will threaten a strike –

With a hell of a shout
Then it's "Out! brothers, out!"

Trade unions may have been necessary in the bad old days of the nineteenth century, it is argued, but in their present form they have long outlived their usefulness. Their powers ought now to be curtailed.

However, some at least of those who study trade unions see them in quite a different light. They believe that the unions in Britain, far from being too powerful, are not powerful enough.

Where does the truth really lie? Are the unions really in need of drastic reform? And, if so, what changes should be made? Has the British trade union movement, the oldest trade union movement in the world, become too insular in outlook and has it a great deal to learn from trade unions in other countries? These are some of the questions which we hope to answer.

THE GROWTH OF THE UNIONS

The British trade union movement is the oldest in the world and, largely because of this, it is also the most complex. There are in Britain a very large number of unions, of many varying types.

The earliest modern unions, formed in the nineteenth century, were unions of skilled workers in particular crafts. These were usually called craft unions. They worked out what hours their members were to work and what wages they were to receive, and would not allow them to work for any employer who would not agree to these conditions. They also carefully regulated the terms by which apprentices were admitted to the craft. By restricting the number of apprentices, they restricted the number of craftsmen. In this way, they ensured that the union members could command higher wages than those paid to workers outside the unions and also that they were less likely to be unemployed.

Towards the end of the century, manual workers began to form unions. These were often unions of all the manual workers in a particular industry and are therefore known as industrial unions.

Later on, in the twentieth century, unions were formed which recruited members freely from more than one industry and these are known as general unions. The two largest unions in Britain, the Transport and General Workers' Union (TGWU) and the General and Municipal Workers' Union (GMWU), are of this kind.

Some unions began as unions of workers following a particular occupation or trade and then succeeded in absorbing other occupational unions. An example is the Electrical Electronic Telecommunications and Plumbing Union (EETPU).

There are yet other unions, such as the Union of Shop Distributive and Allied Workers (USDAW), which recruit largely similar kinds of workers but from a wide variety of industries.

Besides the manual workers' unions, there have sprung up a number of unions of non-manual workers, the so-called white-collar unions.

Some industrial unions, for example the National Union of Mineworkers (NUM), work alongside separate maintenance and white-collar unions in the same industry. A similar picture is true in the steel and railway industries.

Altogether, the situation is a very complicated one indeed.

And just as there are many differing kinds of unions, there are also in Britain a large number of unions, some large and powerful and some very small indeed. In 1975 there were as many as 488 registered unions and the average size of unions was 24,000 members. Eleven large unions had over 250,000 members each and together they had 60% of the total union membership. At the other end of the scale, there were 77 unions with fewer than 100 members each.

Rather more than 50% of all the workers in Britain are trade union members. This is a higher proportion than in most other major European countries, with the exception of Sweden.

Trade union membership has grown quite rapidly since 1960. This is in some ways a surprise, because the number of workers employed in long-established, heavy industries has declined dramatically and it was in these industries that most trade union members used to be found.

The decline in heavy industries has been reflected in a decline in membership of the National Union of Mineworkers and the National Union of Railwaymen. In 1960 the NUM had 638,988 members and was the fourth largest union. By 1976 it had only 261,871 members and was only the tenth largest union. In 1960 the NUR had 333,844 members and was the sixth largest union. By 1976 it had 180,429 members and was the thirteenth largest union.

The brushmakers' union, like other early unions, was ➤ careful to control the number of members admitted.

THE TRADE EXPECTS EVERY MAN TO DO HIS DUTY

BRUSH MAKERS CERTIFICATE.

This is to certify that the Bearer

has served his legal Apprenticeship to

Mr Clark & Burbidge of Leicester (and

came out of his time 25th Sept 1830

Issued at Leicester Signed by

Senior Members	Stewards
Shuttleworth	Francis Cooke
Thos Jesson	Wm Wuduston
Wm Cook	Robt Webb Sec

The membership card of a manual workers' union.

BE UNITED AND INDUSTRIOUS

AMALGAMATED SOCIETY OF ENGINEERS, MACHINISTS, MILLWRIGHTS, SMITHS, AND PATTERN MAKERS.

This is to Certify that _____ was admitted a Member of the _____ Branch on the _____ day of _____ 18__. In witness whereof we have subscribed our names and affixed the Society's Seal

PRESIDENT   SECRETARY

While the number of workers in manufacturing industry has declined, there has been a great increase in the number of workers in local government and in the health and education services. More and more of these workers have joined the trade unions. The Confederation of Health Service Employees (COHSE) has grown from 64,000 in 1964 to 200,000 members in 1976, an increase of 160%. The National and Local Government Officers Association (NALGO) has grown from 338,000 members in 1964 to 690,000 in 1977 and it is now the fifth largest union.

The number of persons employed in central government has also increased, partly because both Conservative and Labour governments have encouraged government employees to join unions. It is now estimated that 85% of central government workers are trade union members.

As a result of these developments, the number of workers in unions affiliated to the TUC (the confederation of British trade unions to which most unions belong) has risen from 8 million in 1952 to 11½ million in 1977.

Many owners and managers in the private sector of industry have been opposed to their office workers joining unions, but here again trade union membership has grown. The union which is now called the Association of Scientific, Technical and Managerial Staffs (ASTMS) had 420,000 members in 1977.

This rapid growth in trade union membership has taken place despite the fact that a great many people have a very low opinion of trade unions, blaming them for all the country's economic difficulties.

Why has this happened? One answer seems to be that an increasing number of workers have come to believe that they cannot afford not to belong to a union. At a time of rapid inflation and increasing direct taxation, they feel that only a strong union can secure the increased wages that are necessary to maintain their standard of living.

Another cause of trade union growth has been the increasing number of women who have joined trade unions. This is partly because the number of married

Demonstrating, March 1980.

women going out to work has increased very considerably. In 1931 only 10% of married women went out to work. By 1971 the figure had become 42%. By 1974, of the increased numbers of women in work, no less than 47% were union members.

Union membership has also been boosted in recent years by the spreading institution of the closed shop. A closed shop exists where only union members can hold jobs in a certain industry. This practice has led to many workers becoming union members, although they may have little sympathy with the union's aims.

Another reason is that in recent years there has been a tendency for smaller firms to be swallowed up by larger ones. Usually, far fewer workers in smaller firms are union members. In 1977 the Bullock Report on trade unions reported that in firms of over 2000 workers 70% of employees on average belonged to a union, while in firms of under 2000 workers only 20% on average belonged to a union.

It has been argued that workers in a large, impersonal firm feel insecure and threatened by management and so find it necessary to join a union. In smaller firms, where the relations between management and workers are more personal and friendly, the workers are less likely to feel this need. Another argument is that most of the managers and owners of small firms are more hostile to trade unions than managers of large firms and they are also in a much better position to discourage workers from joining unions.

TRADE UNION FINANCE

Many British trade unions are large, but they are not necessarily very powerful. This is possibly because British trade unions are generally under-financed and therefore under-manned. The number of full-time paid union officials is small – under 3000 for the whole country. A survey made in 1970 showed that most trade union officials came from the working class. Seventy per cent of them had left school when they were sixteen. Most of them had been shop stewards (unpaid union organizers elected in the workplace) before becoming paid officials. Almost all of them had heavy work loads and worked long hours. Usually, they had little formal training for the work they had to do. Generally, trade union officials are enthusiastic and dedicated.

Most trade union income comes from the subscription fees paid by members. In 1974 the average contribution was £7 per annum or 13 pence per week. This is very little, especially compared with subscriptions paid in most other industrialized countries. The TUC calculated that it "took a man 7 minutes and a woman 12 minutes to earn the weekly contribution". Some unions, however, are much better off than the average and charge higher subscriptions.

The total financial assets of British unions were estimated to be £346,064,000 (1980). In 1975 about £190 million was kept available for strikes and emergencies. Unions receive only about 10% of their income from investments. They usually invest in government stock or local government stock. They are reluctant to invest in private industry. By contrast, Swedish unions have begun a policy of investing heavily in private industry, with the aim of becoming substantial shareholders in industry and so exercising an important influence on how companies are run.

In certain industries employers have been willing to operate the so-called "check-off" system. This means that the employer deducts the union membership fee from the wages of each union member. In this way, the collection of union subscriptions is made easy and far more workers pay their union fees than if they were collected directly by the union.

Certain unions where the employers operate this system, and other unions, which dominate a single industry, along with some of the older craft unions, are quite prosperous. The NUM, for instance, had assets of £26,379,000 in 1980. But other unions, including some of the very big ones and many of the white-collar unions, which compete fiercely with each other for members and so tend to keep their subscriptions low, have small reserves of capital.

The unions spend most of their income on administration and this is despite the fact that they are under-staffed. If they become involved in industrial disputes, they may have to spend large sums of money in strike pay to their members. Because of this, unions are not usually willing to call official strikes except for good reasons. The unions provide legal services to their members, usually to enable them to fight cases of alleged wrongful dismissal, industrial injury or sickness. It is calculated that half a million union members are involved in industrial accidents each year, but only a fifth of them are ever reported. In one year the unions may secure as much as £20 million for their members in compensation.

THE TUC

The TUC (Trades Union Congress) is the federation to which most British trade unions belong. Because of this, it is often seen as being a very powerful institution. It is true that the TUC has exercised great influence over government, at least until the Conservative government of Mrs Thatcher. TUC members have met with the government and employers' representatives to discuss and decide the nation's industrial policy.

The TUC has often worked to persuade the unions to accept the government's policy of restraining wage increases.

Outside the TUC building in London, Len Murray (second from left, front row) stands with trade union officials from many countries, attending the 53rd Industrial Relations Course for Overseas Trade Unionists in 1978.

However, in 1971, the TUC challenged the Conservative government of Edward Heath over the Industrial Relations Act, which the government had passed, and succeeded in making it unworkable.

Under this act, the unions were called upon to place their names on a government register of trade unions. If they refused to do so, they forfeited all the legal rights and privileges of trade unions. But the rights they were to have under the act were considerably less than they had had before.

At the 1971 TUC Congress, a resolution was passed, calling on the unions not to register. It was passed by 5½ million votes to 4½ million – which revealed that a very substantial number of trade unionists did not want to fight the government. Twenty unions did register and were expelled from

Two former General Secretaries: George Woodcock (left) and Vic Feather (right).

the TUC. Later they were re-admitted to membership.

Much to the disappointment of the government, most employers preferred to have nothing to do with the act. In order to maintain good industrial relations within their companies, they continued dealing with the unions whether or not they had registered. Soon, the act was a dead letter and the next government, a Labour one, passed new Industrial Relations Acts, in 1974 and 1975, which made legal once more all the old trade union powers and added new ones.

But the TUC has influence rather than power. It is a confederation of almost all the trade unions of the country, but it has no direct power over the separate unions. "The TUC," said Len Murray, its General Secretary in the early 1980s, "is primarily concerned with developing policy . . . it identifies things which unions should be doing . . . and stimulates them to take the necessary action." The main sanction the TUC has against member unions is expulsion. It cannot impose fines on unions which act in defiance of its agreed policies.

The weakness of the TUC can be seen over the question of encouraging industrial unions. As long ago as 1924, the TUC tried to lead the unions in the direction of having a pattern of trade unionism where the workers in each industry would all belong to one union. Repeated attempts have been made since 1924, especially during the general secretaryship of George Woodcock (1960-69), but they have all met with little success. There are too many large, strong unions, some of them general unions, which have resisted any changes.

But if the TUC has been weak in making change happen, it has been strong in resisting change. The TUC, under Vic Feather, successfully resisted Harold Wilson's proposed Industrial Relations Bill of 1969, which would have made strikes much more difficult.

The effectiveness of the TUC depends very much on the General Secretary. He has a great deal of status, but not much power. His influence depends largely on his personality and powers of persuasion.

Len Murray, the General Secretary in the early 1980s, was a grammar school boy and an Oxford graduate. Most of his working life has been spent in the TUC. In 1954 he was made head of the TUC Economic Department and in 1969 he became Vic

11

THE 80s NOT B

Speakers at the TUC demonstration against the Employment Bill in March 1980: (left to right) Alan Sapper (ACTT), Moss Evans (TGWU), David Basnett (GMWU), Tom Jackson (UPW), Len Murray, Clive Jenkins (ASTMS) and Bill Sirs (ISTC).

Feather's deputy. Like his predecessors in office, he has found it almost impossible to make any radical changes in the workings of the TUC. To achieve anything at all, he has to retain the confidence of the big and powerful unions, by persuasion and making concessions.

The most powerful body in the TUC is the 41-strong General Council. Its composition has come in for much criticism. The Council tends to be dominated by a few large unions, but some large unions have often had no representation on it. Clive Jenkins of the ASTMS has expressed himself with characteristic wit on the subject:

The present groupings are the reflection of a ghostly membership of long-dead trade unionists. What we have is a muddle which is based on ancient patterns of nineteenth century trade and organization, a pattern of industrial archaeology.

The TUC Economic Department produces an annual economic review just before the annual government budget. It is an assessment of the country's economic situation and, when a Conservative government is in power, usually puts forward counter-proposals to government policies. When a Labour government is in power, the review is usually worked out in close co-operation with the government and is broadly in support of government policies.

The TUC Economic Department has only a small staff, like the TUC in general. This is because the TUC, in contrast to trade union confederations abroad, is under-financed. The income of the TUC is only 1½% of the total income of all trade unions. It comes from an annual affiliation fee paid by all trade union members. In 1983 the fee was 47½ pence per member.

The TUC is run through committees. The most important of these is the Finance and General Purposes Committee. The Economic and the International Committees are highly respected, but the Education Committee does not seem to be. In Britain the trade union movement spends very little on the education of its officers and members, compared with what is spent in other countries. On average, a trade union official gets only one and a half days of training per year. This means that even such important work as wage bargaining is often done by unpaid and largely untrained officials. Efforts have recently begun to improve this situation.

WOMEN AND THE TRADE UNIONS

With the growth of the factory system in the nineteenth century, increasing numbers of women were employed in industry outside the home. Craft unions were the dominant form of trade union at the time, and, for the most part, they excluded women from membership.

In 1874 the Women's Protective and Provident League was formed. It was the brainchild of Mrs Emma Paterson. She was a headmaster's daughter and well-educated, but on the death of her father when she was only sixteen, she was forced to earn her own living. She came to realize that there were a great many poorly paid and badly treated women workers in industry, who were in need of trade union protection.

On honeymoon in the United States, she made contact with a number of flourishing women's trade unions there and was impressed by them – especially by the Female Umbrella-Makers' Union of New York. Encouraged by her husband, a trade union secretary, she decided to devote herself to women's trade unionism in Britain.

A number of women's unions, called discreetly "societies", were set up to form the League. Their aims were limited and strike action was ruled out. One important achievement was that the women's unions won the right to be represented at the newly-formed Trades Union Congress founded in 1868.

But there was a great deal of opposition to women's unions and even to women working in industry at all. In 1877 the Trades Union Congress placed it on record that it was

the duty of men and husbands to bring about a condition of things when their wives would be in their proper sphere at home instead of being dragged into competition of livelihood with the great and strong men of the world.

The Women's Protective and Provident League was later renamed the Women's Trade Union League. It campaigned forcefully, over a long period, about the terrible conditions in the pottery trades. Here, because of the glazing processes then in use, both male and female workers were exposed to the danger of lead poisoning. It was not until 1922, however, that effective legislation was passed to improve conditions.

1889 was the year of the famous and controversial

A membership card for a separate women's "society".

**Members of the Matchmakers' Union on strike outside
Bryant and May's, 1888**.

Annie Besant.

match girls' strike at Bryant and May's East End match factory. Many of the girls there suffered from the notorious "phossy jaw", which was gangrene of the mouth and jaw due to phosphorous poisoning. Annie Besant, a member of a middle-class socialist group called the Fabians, and editor of a journal called *Link*, visited the factory and persuaded some of the girls to give information about their pay and conditions. The employers retaliated by sacking the girls concerned. The rest of the workers – 1400 of them – came out on strike. Annie Besant, with the help of the Women's Trade Union League, formed the girls into a union. She also raised subscriptions for strike pay.

The *Times* denounced the strike as the work of socialist agitators. The *Church Times* commented that "no one supposes their wages are satisfactory, but they are ruled by the price they can get for their work".

Eventually, the employers made some concessions and the result was greeted as a great triumph for women unionists. But it was not until 1901 that an act of Parliament was passed which forbade the use of white phosphorous in match making.

The end of the nineteenth century saw the formation of general unions of unskilled workers. These were prepared to admit women to their ranks, on equal terms with men.

Sidney and Beatrice Webb, Fabian socialists and social scientists, estimated that by 1890 there were 100,000 women trade unionists and that by 1907 there were 200,000. The registrar of friendly societies recorded that in 1914 there were 437,000 women in trade unions, out of a total membership of 4,145,000, a small but significant number.

During the First World War (1914-18) women entered industry in large numbers, to replace the men who went into the armed services, and to increase war production. Women's trade union membership trebled.

At the end of the war many women, of course, left industry. They were actively encouraged to do so. A conference of trade unionists and employers in Bristol stated that "women should as a matter of course relinquish jobs in which they have replaced men . . . so long as the men are available to fill them."

The number of women trade unionists declined during the inter-war years, as did trade union membership generally, because of economic depression. It was not to pick up again until the years of rearmament and increasing prosperity leading up to the Second World War.

During the Second World War (1939-45) women's membership of the trade unions doubled and by 1943 stood at almost 2 million. Since the war, twice as many women as men have been recruited into the trade unions and today it is estimated that over a quarter of the membership of the Trades Union Congress is female (2,772,000 out of a total membership of 10,250,000).

This great increase of women's membership in trade unions has come about partly because of union recruitment policy, but more because of the growth of types of employment where women tend to find work – for example, local and national government departments, office work generally, and the National Health Service.

But women, it is believed, do not take part in union

Beatrice and Sidney Webb.

Munitions workers in the First World War.

STOP

WE WANT TO WORK

WE WANT TO WORK

activities to at all the extent that their numbers suggest they should. Not many women are union executive officers or full-time officials. This is probably because some women unionists are married and put family responsibilities before union activity.

Women are involved in fewer strikes than men. The industries where women tend to work do not have strong unions, and strikes are not likely to occur and are not really feasible where there is not a strong union. Moreover, it has been argued that most women are more aware of the needs of their families than are their menfolk and are more reluctant to upset their family finances by going on strike.

But women sometimes do go on strike. And they sometimes complain that, when they do, they get little support from their men colleagues.

A notable women's strike of recent times was in 1968, when women sewing-machinists at Ford's Dagenham plant demanded that their work should be re-graded, to give them an extra five pence an hour. They were soon joined on strike by the women at Ford's Halewood plant. The dispute was settled in favour of the women by the intervention of Barbara Castle, then Secretary of State for Productivity in the Labour government. The strike lasted three weeks and was estimated to have cost the company 8 million pounds in lost production.

The Women's Liberation Movement came to the fore in the 1960s and early '70s, demanding equal pay for women, among other things. By 1960 the TUC gave its backing to this. Equal pay in the public services was achieved as early as 1961, but progress elsewhere was slow. The Labour Party had adopted the principle of "equal pay for equal work" but, when in office, did nothing about it. Wishing above all else to curb inflation and avoid undue wage increases, it was unsympathetic.

Frank Cousins, general secretary of the Transport and General Workers' Union in the 1960s, certainly one of the most powerful union leaders of the day, came out in support of women's demands:

In a technological age, if ever there was an

These women had been laid off work at the Lucas factory in Birmingham for nine weeks, by the strike of toolmakers there (1977). They were allowed to put their case to the men's shop stewards' meeting. How true is it that women are less prepared to strike than men?

Barbara Castle, 1968.

argument that ought to be thrown away by us, it is the one that there is such a thing as women's work.

He demanded "equal pay for work of equal value for all people employed". In 1970 Parliament passed the Equal Pay Act. Women were not wholly satisfied with it, because they thought it too limited in scope.

Women were soon demanding far more than equal pay. Their demands were for general social and economic equality. One demand was for equal training and job opportunities. Male trade unionists were not always sympathetic. The male members of the Transport and General Workers' Union bitterly opposed the re-training as bus drivers of conductresses threatened with redundancy.

Nevertheless, in 1975, a year named by the United Nations Organization as "International Women's Year", the TUC held a huge march through London and rally in Trafalgar Square, in support of women's rights. More important perhaps, many unions, especially white-collar unions, with many women

19

Frank Cousins, 1967.

members, gradually came to realize that active policies in support of women's claims to equality, especially if they involved successful strike action, would lead to more women wanting to join.

The improvement that there undoubtedly has been in women's working conditions has been achieved largely because of the post-war economic boom. Workers, including women, were very much needed and so their demands had to be met, at least in part. The women's trade union movement, having gained momentum, continued into the 1970s, a period of increasing economic difficulty. With increasing unemployment, further progress is not certain. Even with all the efforts that have been made, women's wages still lag far behind those of men.

TRADE UNIONS AND BRITISH POLITICS

Most trade union movements are closely connected with a left-wing socialist political party, and the British trade union movement is no exception. Indeed, it was the TUC which gave birth to the British Labour Party. In 1900 the TUC created a pressure group in Parliament, a group of MPs who would support the policies of the unions. It was called the Labour Representation Committee and was the beginning of the Labour Party. The links between the trade unions and the Labour Party have remained close ever since, but this does not mean that the two have always seen eye to eye.

In 1945 the electorate returned to power a Labour government, under Clement Attlee, whose policies of nationalization and full employment were whole-heartedly supported by the unions. By 1948, however, the government was running into serious economic difficulties and trying to halt the rapid increase in wages. The unions agreed to voluntary restraint on wage demands. This worked reasonably well for two years, after which a wages explosion took place.

From 1964 onwards the unions were again called upon to make sacrifices for the good of a Labour government. In 1966, after two years of unsuccessfully operating a voluntary wage restraint policy, they agreed to a statutory incomes policy: that is, an incomes policy laid down and operated by government.

When the Conservatives came to power in 1970, relations between unions and government followed a similar pattern. A period of voluntary wage restraint was followed by an attempt by government to enforce a statutory incomes policy. The unions resisted, and the Heath government's incomes policy was one of the main issues in the next general election of 1974, which the Conservatives lost.

In January 1972 the TUC-Labour Party Liaison Committee was formed, to work out future policies. The initiative to form the Committee came mainly from the TUC – especially from Jack Jones, leader of the TGWU. The Committee produced a policy statement calling for control of basic food prices through subsidies; the subsidizing of transport fares (and even experiments in free public transport); public ownership of land for building; a large-scale redistribution of income from rich to poor; the phasing out of charges for doctors' prescriptions and dental treatment; and greatly increased old-age pensions.

When a Labour government was returned to power in 1974, co-operation between the unions and government was very close indeed, and laws were passed strengthening the legal position of the unions. But soon the country ran into economic difficulties. Prices rose by 25% in a single year and wage settlements were even higher. The unions reluctantly accepted a stricter policy of wage restraint. For 1975 they contented themselves with a flat rate increase of £6 per week for all workers. Some low-paid workers benefited more under this arrangement than they had ever done previously.

The unions expected that the government would continue its policies in favour of workers, but unemployment soon rose to over a million, which was then thought unacceptably high, prices remained high, and the government rejected the demand for selective import controls which the TUC believed would solve the country's economic difficulties. In 1976 Dennis Healey, the Chancellor of the Exchequer, negotiated a loan from the International Monetary Fund. In order to secure this loan, he had to agree to make large cuts in public expenditure. Relations between unions and government became strained.

The Conservative government which took power in 1979, under Margaret Thatcher, has rejected the idea of a statutory wages policy, but has called upon the workers to exercise wage restraint in order not to price themselves out of jobs. The government has checked wage rises in the public sector of employment through a tighter control of public

21

The Labour Party and the unions. This picture was taken outside Transport House, where leading members of the Labour Party were going to discuss election strategy in 1979. Tony Benn, holding the official magazine of the TGWU, is talking with members of the Society of Civil and Public Servants.

expenditure. But the most important factor in keeping wage settlements down has been the high level of unemployment. In a time of economic recession and high unemployment, trade unions have very little bargaining power.

The Labour Party is dependent on the unions financially. Unions that are affiliated to the party – in 1976, 59 of the 133 unions in the TUC were affiliated – pay a political levy to the party. Members of these unions who do not support the Labour Party can contract out of paying, but most do not bother to do this. In 1927, just after the General Strike, Baldwin's Conservative government altered the law, making it necessary for trade unionists to contract into paying the levy. As a result, trade union membership in the Labour Party dropped by nearly a million. In 1946 the Labour government reversed the law once more and union membership in the Labour Party rose in one year from just over 2½ million to nearly 4½ million. Obviously, the attitude of a great many union members to the Labour Party is apathetic. In deciding whether or not to pay the levy, they just take the easiest course.

The unions have considerable power in the Labour Party. The leader of each affiliated union can decide which way all the votes of all the union's members should go, at the Labour Party's annual conference. This is the controversial "block-voting system". The unions control 90% of the votes at Labour Party annual conferences. For a long period after the Second World War, most of the trade union leaders were on the right wing of the party and their influence was approved of by the majority of Labour MPs. More recently, the unions have been accused of swinging to the left and union power in the party has come in for much more criticism from MPs and others.

It has been estimated that only about two-thirds of union members usually vote Labour at general elections. This indicates that a great many union members do not share the wider political aspirations of the trade union movement. It is especially true of many of the white-collar unions. Only a third of the members of ASTMS pay the political levy and only a seventh of members of the print union SOGAT (Society of Graphical and Allied Trades).

In contrast, the unions usually loyal to the Labour Party are the general and industrial unions – the TGWU, the GMWU, the miners, railwaymen and electricians.

A great deal has been said and written about the influence of Communist Party members within the unions, suggesting that it is harmful. It is not only some Conservatives who see a small group of Communists as causing almost all the industrial unrest in the country. In 1966 the Labour Prime Minister, Harold Wilson, blamed the seamen's strike of that year on them. In the House of Commons he said that the Communists

have an efficient and disciplined industrial apparatus controlled by headquarters. No major strike occurs anywhere in the country in any sector of industry in which the apparatus does not concern itself.

Is this picture of the Communists really true? Are they really so important in the unions?

As a political party in Britain, the Communists are not very powerful. They have few members – only 30,000 in 1975; their newspaper, the *Morning Star*, has only a small circulation; and they have usually been unsuccessful in gaining seats in Parliament.

But they work hard for their cause and are active in union affairs. In the mid-1970s, it was estimated that possibly 10% of union officials were Communists. They were once especially strong in certain unions and for a time controlled the electrical trades union. But in 1963 they were accused of ballot-rigging in order to remain in power there and were banned from office. In 1972, during the national coal strike, Communists were prominent in the mass picketing of Saltley coal depot, which successfully prevented the moving of coal supplies to power stations. Jimmy Reid and Jimmy Airlie, both Communists, led the work-in at the Upper Clyde Shipyards, which were threatened with closure in the early 1970s.

But Communists cannot create industrial unrest where the workers do not have genuine grievances. If they were seen to be nothing but trouble-makers, their influence with the workers would soon end. If they do believe in the desirability of political revolution, they usually see it as being a long way off. To retain the day-to-day confidence of workmates, Communists must temper their political aims with moderation and common-sense.

TRADE UNIONS AND WORLD POLITICS

We want to see a more peaceful world, a more equal world, where economic progress can be made by working people everywhere. Solidarity, understanding and friendship are the trade union answer to international tension. (Jack Jones, trade union leader)

In the 1930s the British trade union movement was opposed to any appeasement policy being adopted towards Hitler and Mussolini, although it also opposed re-armament. Many trade unionists volunteered to fight against Franco and the nationalist forces in the Spanish Civil War.

Many trade unionists felt some sympathy in the 1930s towards Russia's Communist regime, but the TUC opposed the efforts of Stalin, the Russian dictator, to bring the international trade union movement, the World Federation of Trade Unions, under Russian control. In 1949 the TUC was active in helping to form a rival anti-Communist trade union federation, the International Confederation of Free Trade Unions.

The TUC has always been critical of repressive right-wing governments – for example, in Bolivia, Chile, Argentina and South Africa. Trade unionists have been among the first to suffer from government repression in these countries. The TUC has provided money and support for victims of right-wing oppression.

But British trade unionists, with some notable exceptions, have been reluctant to criticize Communist governments for the way in which they have treated their own trade unions. On a number of occasions, working-class revolt has taken place in Eastern Europe – in East Germany in 1953, in

Jack Jones, 1977.

A certificate presented to the TUC by the ICFTU.

Deeply conscious of the lasting debt which trade unionists of all lands owe to the selfless idealism and unsparing devotion to the cause of Labour of the early pioneers, the Executive Board of the International Confederation of Free Trade Unions presents this testimony to the General Secretary of the British Trades Union Congress, George Woodcock, on the occasion of the hundredth anniversary of the foundation of the TUC
Having blazed a trail for the organised workers of the whole world, and as a loyal and trusty founder member of this Confederation, may the TUC go on from strength to strength in pursuit of that noble aim which we shall always hold in common - social justice for the workers everywhere in conditions of peace and freedom

For the ICFTU Executive Board
Brussels, 3 July 1968
President~   General Secretary

The monument to shipyard workers who were killed in
the 1970 riots in the Lenin Shipyard in Gdansk, Poland.

Shipyard workers on strike in Gdansk, along with relatives and other citizens, knelt in prayer outside the shipyards, August 1980.

May 1983. To disperse Solidarity demonstrators from Warsaw's old town, the police used water cannon and riot clubs.

Hungary in 1956, in Czechoslovakia in 1968, and in the Polish shipyards in 1970, 1976, 1980 and since then, this revolt led by the Solidarity free trade union movement. On each occasion, thousands of workers have been brought to trial. Some have been executed and others imprisoned.

Trade unions in Communist countries are very different from those in the free world. Communist governments believe that trade unions are necessary in capitalist countries, to protect the workers from exploitation by capitalist employers. In Communist countries it is the workers themselves, in theory, acting through the workers' state, who own the industrial undertakings. Clearly, the workers do not need to be protected from themselves. Therefore, the governments believe that unions are no longer necessary.

Unions do exist in Communist countries, but they take on a different and more restricted role than elsewhere. The Communist Party influences the choice of union officers. Union officials are expected to discipline the workers and persuade them to adopt correct and orderly work habits. Unions work closely with management. The managers have far wider powers over the workers than in most western countries. They can take away the workers' bonus payments and reduce pay for bad workmanship. The unions have no legal right to strike and workers found guilty of disrupting work may be deported to labour camps and forced to do hard labour for up to five years. Recently, a number of American-based multi-national companies have set up factories in Eastern Europe because there they can be assured of a docile and well-disciplined work force. Even so, studies by industrial scientists have shown that trade unions in the Soviet Union do play a useful, if rather minor, function in representing workers' interests.

Critics of the TUC think that it ought to have protested more against the ill-treatment of dissidents in the Soviet Union. They argue that it should do more for the struggling unions and workers of the developing countries. TUC demands for import controls and the protection of certain British industries would, if granted, make it more difficult for developing countries to trade. British trade unions are seen as having inward-looking attitudes.

The TUC's hostility to Britain's entry into the

Len Murray and other union leaders helped to load a lorry with supplies for Poland, March 1982.

European Economic Community is seen by many as one more example of insularity. In 1972 the TUC decided to boycott all EEC institutions. This meant that there were no TUC representatives on EEC boards dealing with such matters as the economy and unemployment. The CBI, the British employers' organization, took the places offered to them, and West European trade unionists found themselves out-voted because their British counterparts were not there to vote.

British unions are often accused of being self-satisfied and of feeling that, because of the long history of trade unionism in the country, they have little to learn from trade unions in Western Europe. But, in fact, in an age which has seen the rapid growth of multi-national corporations and other international organizations, it seems only common-sense for trade unionists to co-operate as much as possible across international barriers. However, this is easy to talk about, and much more difficult to achieve.

Certain unions, such as the car workers', miners' and steel workers' unions, have seen the need to establish closer links with unions in Europe. One result of this has been to show British workers how far short their conditions fall of those in Western Europe. Most significantly, wages are usually lower and the length of working life is longer in Britain than in Europe.

SHOP STEWARDS

One aspect of British trade unionism which arouses much controversy is the recent growth in the power and influence of shop stewards. These are the unpaid union officials elected by the workers from among themselves in the workplace. The importance of shop stewards in Britain is without parallel in any other industrial country. In 1975 it was estimated that there were nearly 300,000 shop stewards in Britain, or about one for every 65 trade union members. They are especially important in the engineering and metal industries and in manufacturing industry generally, where most wage settlements are made by shop stewards at factory level.

It is often assumed that shop stewards are likely to be politically motivated extremists, forever stirring up trouble. This may be true of some, but, in fact, most shop stewards, who are unpaid, over-worked and largely untrained, often try hard to avoid taking industrial action. Unless the workers' case is a good one and they feel strongly about it, industrial action is likely to be unpopular. Inter-union committees of stewards in the factories often work to iron out difficulties between unions.

Jack Jones, former head of the TGWU, Britain's largest union, was a firm believer in the desirability of increasing the power of shop stewards:

We have got to get our agreements down to the point where the workers themselves are involved in the negotiations and want to keep them because they have had a decisive hand in making them and therefore understand them.

The TGWU Shop Stewards' Handbook, giving advice to stewards, produced in 1974, has this to say:

When the public at large thinks about us [i.e. the union] they have in mind very often the general secretary. But to the members in our shop the image the union will conjure up will certainly be you. Make sure you are a good advertisement. The way to do this is to carry out efficiently your job as a shop steward.

The Donovan Commission which reported on trade unions in 1968 said that

stewards are rarely agitators pushing workers towards unconstitutional action . . . quite commonly they are supporters of order exercising a restraining influence on their members.

Many managers seem to agree with this, preferring to deal with the stewards within the company than with full-time union officials from outside. It has been suggested that the practice of workplace bargaining works to the advantage of the management, because the negotiations are more easily limited to pay and conditions than if they were made at company or industry level. Here the scope of negotiations would tend to be widened to include such things as redundancy agreements and company pension schemes.

The author of a recent book on British trade unions writes of shop stewards:

Fred Kite, played by Peter Sellers, in *I'm All Right Jack* [a satirical film], is the stereotype steward of popular imagination – Bone-headed, sanctimonious, humourless, a stickler for the blessed rule-book and a formidable obstacle to industrial progress. Nothing could be further from the truth. (from *The Fifth Estate, Britain's Unions in the Seventies* by Robert Taylor, Routledge & Kegan Paul Ltd, 1978).

NEW TECHNOLOGY AND THE UNIONS

Great prominence is given in the media to recent developments in micro-electronics. A new technology is coming into being, it is said, whose consequences will be just as momentous as those of the industrial revolution of the eighteenth and nineteenth centuries. But the pace of change will be infinitely more rapid. What can unions do to profit and not suffer from the changes?

Briefly, micro-electronics is the miniaturization of electronic circuitry. A quarter of a million electronic components can now be put into a single silicon chip the size of a thumb-nail and costing only a few pounds. Even this degree of miniaturization will soon be outdated by further reductions in size.

In the office and in the factory, machinery takes the place of human workers.

Electronic circuits housed in silicon chips can be grouped together to form micro-processors which are really miniaturized computers.

The first electronics industry in the world grew up in the 1960s in the United States, because of the needs of the space exploration programme. The USA still leads the world in producing micro-electronic components, accounting for 70% of world output. Its only serious rival is Japan. In Britain, the infant micro-electronics industry concentrates largely on programming new computer systems (often called software), and in this field British skills are rated as among the best in the world.

One important effect of the introduction of micro-electronic technology, which concerns unions, will be on jobs. Computer-controlled machines and

robots may replace craftsmen, machine-operators and assemblers in factories. New automated office equipment will make many routine office jobs redundant. We do not know yet how many new jobs will be created to replace those that will be lost, but there is some danger of unemployment connected with these changes.

How ought the trade unions to react to the impending changes? One way might be to oppose changes by strike action or other methods. But past historical examples of workers who opposed change, such as the Luddites who smashed machines during the industrial revolution, suggest that trying to halt progress would be counter-productive.

The TUC recognizes this and in a report called *Employment and Technology*, produced in 1979, firmly stated that it accepts and even welcomes the changes. But it does believe that the changes must be controlled by government, trade unions, and management, in such a way that they do not bring prosperity to one section of the people and poverty and unemployment to another.

As Len Murray writes in a foreword to the report:

It is not just a question of accepting the new technology or of fighting it. The issue is how we can maximise its benefits and minimize its costs, and ensure that its benefits are equitably shared. The new technology has been described as "the second industrial revolution". We have to ensure that unlike the first industrial revolution, this second revolution now upon us will not trample underfoot the welfare and interests of those directly affected in the process of change.

The TUC believes that the benefits of the new technology should be used to enable workers to lead more satisfying lives and not be so tied to work. It says: "At every stage technological change should be linked with a reduction in the working week, working year and working life-time". Trade unionists negotiating new technology agreements should try to secure increased leisure for the workers. The report says:

Priority should be given to movement towards:
the 35-hour week,
a reduction in systematic overtime,
longer holidays,
better provision for time-off for public and trade union duties,
sabbatical leave, and
early retirement for older workers on improved pensions.

But, to many people, these aspirations seem unrealistic. They argue that, at a time of economic difficulty, a reduction of the working week would only increase the costs of production and thus delay progress. Thus, the introduction of the changes the TUC wants may come only in the distant future.

THE EFFECTIVENESS OF BRITISH TRADE UNIONS

How effective are British trade unions in achieving their declared aims, the betterment of pay and conditions for their members? And do they have too much power in trying to achieve these aims?

Unions differ a great deal in how much pressure they can exert to achieve better pay settlements. Some industrial workers – such as the miners or the power workers – can have an immediate, disastrous effect on the economy and people's lives if they go on strike. They have often used this power to become very highly paid: this industrial "muscle power" is one of the reasons why the miners are among the best-paid industrial workers in the country. Their long tradition of struggle and solidarity among themselves is another.

Other groups of workers – such as the teachers or the nurses – have traditionally been unwilling to go on strike, because they believe they offer a service which should not be withdrawn. It is argued that the government tends to use these people's reluctance to go on strike, to avoid paying them large wage increases.

Most wage bargaining in all industries takes place during the winter, from November to April, setting wage levels for the following year. The pay agreements have different starting and finishing dates, and one group of workers will be influenced by what it sees another group to have achieved. But many different percentage increases are achieved, depending on the bargaining power of workers and the prosperity of employers, and some workers and unionists believe the whole system is arbitrary and unfair.

Two strikes which affected the general public were the water and sewerage workers' strike in January 1983 and the hospital doctors' strike in 1975.

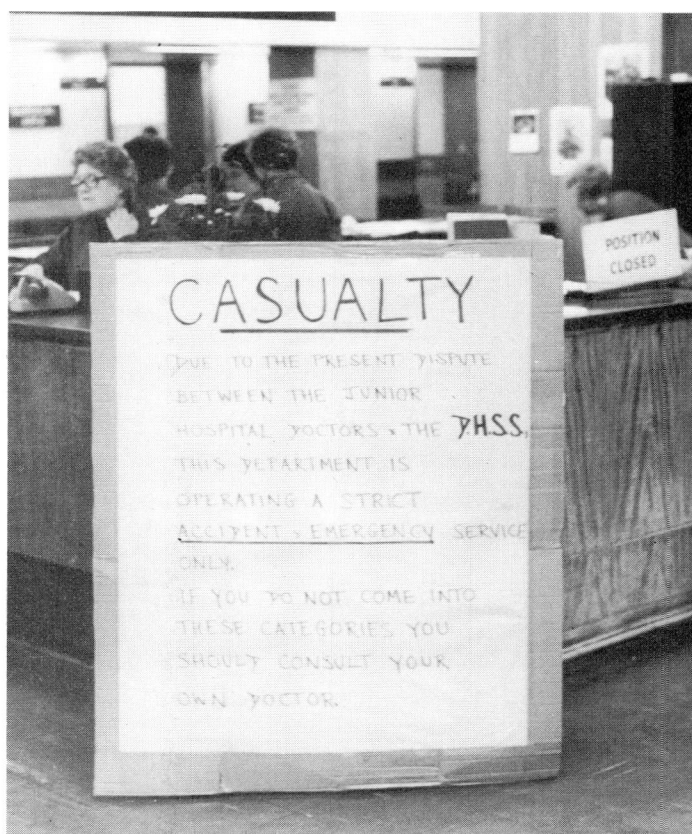

CASUALTY

DUE TO THE PRESENT DISPUTE BETWEEN THE JUNIOR HOSPITAL DOCTORS & THE D.H.S.S. THIS DEPARTMENT IS OPERATING A STRICT ACCIDENT & EMERGENCY SERVICE ONLY. IF YOU DO NOT COME INTO THESE CATEGORIES YOU SHOULD CONSULT YOUR OWN DOCTOR.

NATIONAL UNION OF JOURNALISTS

Acorn House, 314 Gray's Inn Road, London WC1X 8DP
Telephone: 01-278 7916

CODE OF PROFESSIONAL CONDUCT

Like other trade unions, formed for mutual protection and economic betterment, the National Union of Journalists desires and encourages its members to maintain good quality of workmanship and high standards of conduct.

Through years of courageous struggle for better wages and working conditions its pioneers and their successors have kept these aims in mind, and have made provision in Union rules not only for penalties on offenders, but for the guidance and financial support of members who may suffer loss of work for conforming to Union principles.

While punishment by fine, suspension or expulsion is provided for in cases of "conduct detrimental to the interests of the Union or of the profession," any member who is victimised (Rule 20, clause (g)) for refusing to do work . . . "incompatible with the honour and interests of the profession," may rely on adequate support from Union funds.

A member of the Union has two claims on his loyalty—one by his Union and one by his employer. These need not clash so long as the employer complies with the agreed Union conditions and makes no demand for forms of service incompatible with the honour of the profession or with the principles of trade unionism.

1. A member should do nothing that would bring discredit on himself, his Union, his newspaper, or his profession. He should study the rules of his Union, and should not, by commission or omission, act against the interests of the Union.

2. Unless the employer consents to a variation, a member who wishes to terminate his employment must give notice, according to agreement or professional custom.

3. No member should seek promotion or seek to obtain the position of another journalist by unfair methods.

4. A member should not, directly or indirectly, attempt to obtain for himself or anyone else any commission, regular or occasional, held by a freelance member of the Union. A member should not accept a commission normally held by a freelance member of the Union without reasonable cause.

5. It is unprofessional conduct to exploit the labour of another journalist by plagiarism, or by using his copy for linage purposes without permission.

6. Staff men who do linage work should be prepared to give up such work to conform with any pooling scheme approved by the N.E.C., or any Union plan to provide a freelance member with a means of earning a living.

7. A member holding a staff appointment shall serve first the paper that employs him. In his own time a member is free to engage in other creative work, but he should not undertake any extra work in his rest time or holidays if by so doing he is depriving an out-of-work member of a chance to obtain employment. Any misuse of rest days—won by the Union on the sound argument that periods of recuperation are needed after strenuous hours of labour—is damaging to trade union aims for a shorter working week.

8. While a spirit of willingness to help other members should be encouraged at all times, members are under a special obligation of honour to help an unemployed member to obtain work.

9. Every journalist should treat subordinates as considerately as he would desire to be treated by his superiors.

10. Freedom in the honest collection and publication of news facts, and the rights of fair comment and criticism, are principles which every journalist should defend.

11. A journalist should fully realise his personal responsibility for everything he sends to his paper or agency. He should keep Union and professional secrets, and respect all necessary confidences regarding sources of information and private documents. He should not falsify information or documents, or distort or misrepresent facts.

12. In obtaining news or pictures, reporters and Press photographers should do nothing that will cause pain or humiliation to innocent, bereaved, or otherwise distressed persons. News, pictures, and documents should be acquired by honest methods only.

13. Every journalist should keep in mind the dangers in the laws of libel, contempt of court, and copyright. In reports of law court proceedings it is necessary to observe and practise the rule of fair play to all parties.

14. Whether for publication or suppression, the acceptance of a bribe by a journalist is one of the gravest professional offences.

15. A journalist shall not, in the performance of his professional duties, lend himself to the distortion or suppression of the truth because of advertising considerations.

16. Except in the case of freelances, reporters should not take photographs and photographers should not report, other than in exceptional circumstances.

September, 1973

Belonging to a union brings benefits and responsibilities.

Nevertheless, most trade unionists believe in the present system, which is called free collective bargaining. This means that each union negotiates freely with employers on behalf of the workers in the union, and without restriction on the level of settlement that can be achieved. The opposite to this is a statutory incomes policy, where the level of increases is laid down by the government. This is usually a percentage increase, but there was a brief period – from 1975 to 1977 – when the unions accepted a wage restraint policy that took the form of a flat-rate increase which was the same for all workers. Lower-paid workers did well under this scheme, but it was disliked by some workers and unionists who felt that differentials (different wage rates for different types and skills of job) ought to be maintained.

The unions prefer collective bargaining to incomes policy because they believe that an incomes policy is often a means of holding wages down, and also perhaps because they are suspicious of being regulated by the law and the courts. Governments have been in favour of incomes policies at various periods, but some governments are suspicious of them because they become impossible to enforce and are felt to restrict what industry can do.

The most important reason why an incomes policy is introduced is as a control on inflation – rising prices and costs. The unions are sometimes blamed for inflation, because the cost of the large wage settlements on which they often insist has to be met by higher prices for industry's goods. Economists differ as to whether high wage settlements are the main cause of inflation.

Trade unions have been successful in helping certain groups of workers to become highly-paid, but it is often argued that they have failed lower-paid workers, many of whom would undoubtedly be better-off claiming social security benefits than working. The wages of the lower-paid are in theory controlled by government-appointed bodies called wages councils, covering 3 million low-paid workers. But in practice these bodies have been unable to improve pay and conditions much for the workers they try to help. Sometimes these are in industries where unions are not strong, but, even where there are unions, workers may suffer from the fact that they have little "muscle power" under the system of free collective bargaining. In 1974 Alan Fisher of NUPE (National Union of Public Employees) called for a national minimum wage to be set at the beginning of each pay round, but the TUC was unwilling to support this.

It is also sometimes argued that, while trade unions may have been successful in winning high pay settlements for some groups of workers, they have damaged the country by enforcing high wages where levels of production and productivity did not justify it and by enforcing restrictive practices and resisting change in an effort to save jobs. These charges are, of course, hotly denied by trade unionists, but it is possible to give a list of industries – such as the shipbuilding or film industries – where trade union practices do seem to have played a part in making the industry uncompetitive. Other workers – such as the miners – have often co-operated, however, in modernization programmes, even where this meant loss of jobs.

Another area where the performance of British unions has been questioned is the area of conditions, as opposed to pay. More than in many other countries, British unions have tended to concentrate on levels of wages, workers have voted for or against settlements mainly on wage grounds, and conditions have sometimes been forgotten. The trade unions have long been calling for longer holiday periods and earlier retirement, but they have had little success in enforcing these demands. Unions have also been active in calling for higher safety standards in industry, and the 1974 Health and Safety at Work Act was a union-inspired measure which appointed government inspectors to tour factories and check on safety. Even so, there are still around 500,000 industrial accidents each year which keep workers away from work for more than three days, and every year around 300 workers are killed at work.

In many ways, it seems that unions in Britain, despite their long history, great size and past achievements, are not as successful at improving life for workers as unions abroad, and this has led TUC leader Len Murray to argue that, far from the unions being too powerful, they are not powerful enough. Others argue that unions in Britain are powerful, but do not use their power for the right ends. The question remains highly controversial.

TRADE UNIONS AND STRIKES

Great public concern is often expressed about the large number of strikes that, rightly or wrongly, are believed to take place in Britain. Britain is sometimes compared with other countries – West Germany, in particular – where strikes are thought to be very rare occurrences. Some people believe that workers are always ready to down tools at the slightest provocation and over the most trivial issues – the length of tea breaks, or demarcation disputes (that is, disputes between different groups of workers as to who does what work).

The large number of strikes in Britain is often considered an important, if not the most important reason, for the country's poor economic performance. Even the Donovan Commission on Trade Unions, in its influential report in 1968, said:

> We have no hesitation in saying that the prevalence of unofficial strikes and their tendency to increase has such serious economic implications that measures to deal with them are urgently needed.

Recently, a long and crippling strike has occurred in the steel industry, a major industry previously known for its long history of good industrial relations. Groups of workers who it was thought would never or ought never to go on strike, such as the nurses, the hospital workers, the ambulance men, even the highly paid hospital consultants (surgeons and physicians), have gone on strike. How can better industrial relations be achieved?

Obviously, a strike is a very serious matter and can damage the public in general, as well as other firms, which may suffer losses and lose orders, which in turn may lead to other groups of workers losing their jobs.

The belief that Britain is strike-ridden is widely held not only in Britain but also overseas. In foreign newspapers, the large number of strikes in Britain is often referred to as the "British Disease". Foreign investors may be reluctant to invest in Britain and

April 1983. British Leyland workers were on strike about the management proposal to phase out the five-minute "washing-up time" which the workers were allowed at the end of each shift.

Steelworkers on strike, 1980.

foreign buyers to place orders with British firms because of this belief.

The trade unions are never voluntarily going to give up the right to strike. They argue that without the right to threaten strike action, and if necessary to actually take it, they would have little power in bargaining with employers. There is evidence that this is true. In jobs where workers are scattered thinly over a wide area, as in agriculture; or where many of the workers are women, or only work part-time; or where there is a generally held belief that to take strike action is morally wrong, as in nursing for example – in all such jobs, where it is difficult or sometimes impossible for trade unions to organize effective strike action, wages and salaries are much lower than those in trades and professions where strike action is more easily possible.

Not many people would want to take away from workers the right to strike. But a great many people do want to make it more difficult for workers to strike. They would like to outlaw all unofficial strikes (those strikes that do not have union support). They would like to make sure that all strikes are supported out of union funds rather than through the payment of unemployment or social security benefits to strikers and their families.

However, Britain is not alone in suffering the ill-effects of strikes. It is difficult to compare the statistics supplied by different countries on the frequency of strikes, as all countries do not compile their statistics in the same way. Some countries, for instance, do not record strikes that last only a short time, or those which involve fewer than a certain number of people, or those which do not have official union support. But one recent survey says that "we [Britain] are placed sixth or seventh among the 15 countries for which adequate information is available, which in relative terms makes us average rather than bad." (*Strikes in Britain*, C.T.B. Smith et al, HMSO, 1978)

Workers at one steel plant in Sheerness refused to join ▶ the national steel strike in 1980. Other steel workers came to picket the plant. Wives of the Sheerness workers offered their advice.

British Foreign Office staff, members of the Civil Service Unions, form a picket line in Downing Street, during a 24-hour national stoppage in support of a pay claim.

Research has shown that an average worker in Britain is involved in strike action only once each ten years. But strikes are not spread evenly throughout industry. The frequency of strikes in any industry will vary from year to year, but generally speaking, the most troubled industries are mining, transport, engineering, motor car manufacture and docks. The same pattern is true of other countries.

It can be argued, on the one hand, that since Britain is more dependent than other nations on overseas trade, to have an average level of strikes is not good enough. Britain cannot afford to lag behind its competitors, such as West Germany and Japan.

On the other hand, it can be said that the black picture often painted of industrial relations in Britain is not only grossly unfair, but also very damaging to the country's image abroad and to its performance in overseas trade.

It is often thought that strikes are much more frequent in certain areas of the country than in others. Merseyside is often picked out as a black spot. This may be slightly unfair.

Much more important, in fact, than the area of the country is the size of the industrial undertaking.

Police and press (notice the microphone) both ▶ watched over the British Leyland pickets who stopped and talked to management staff arriving at their Longbridge plant in Birmingham, November 1981.

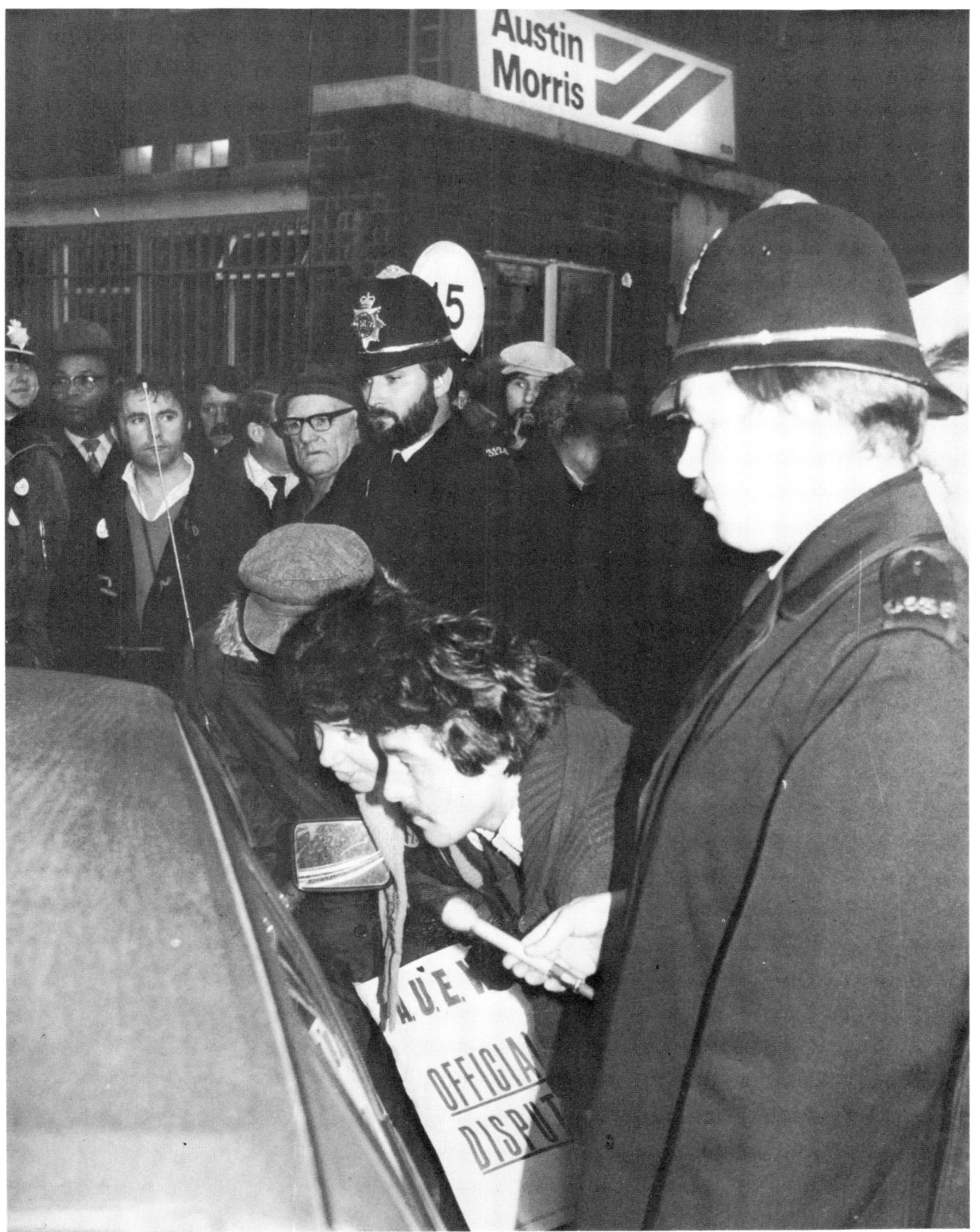

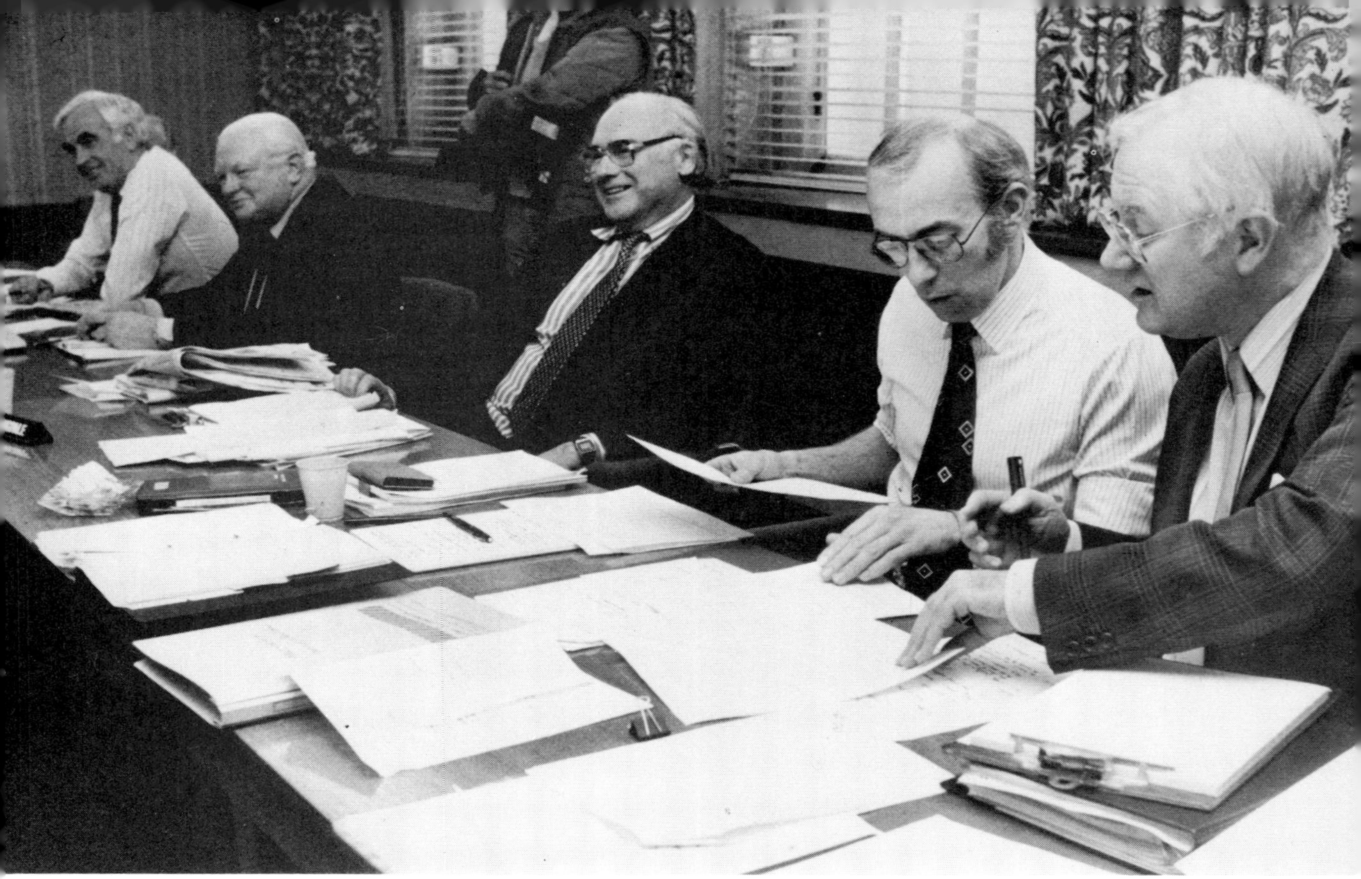

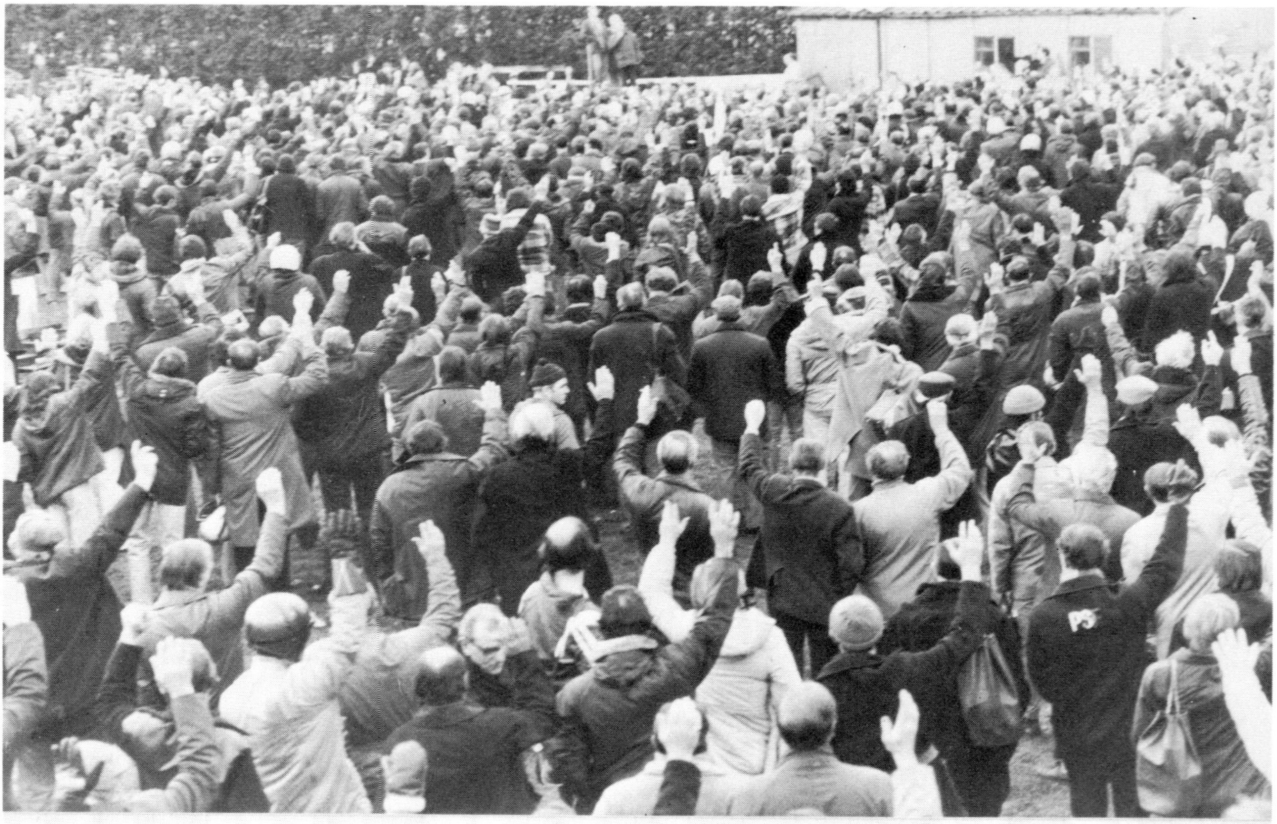

Strikes tend to happen in large firms and only in a small number even of these. Small firms tend to be almost entirely strike-free, perhaps because communication is easier and relationships closer.

We have mentioned the belief that most strikes are about unimportant issues, especially about who does what. In fact, only about one in a hundred stoppages arise from demarcation disputes. The overwhelming majority of strikes are about pay and conditions and job security.

Some writers on industrial affairs believe that the ill-effects of even major strikes have been exaggerated. After a strike, especially a successful one, workers often achieve higher productivity than normal and lost production is made up.

A general conclusion might be that, while strikes may, indeed, be very damaging to the country, they are probably over-estimated as a cause of industrial and trading problems.

◄ British Leyland workers voting to go back to work.

GRUNWICK~AN EXAMPLE OF AN INDUSTRIAL DISPUTE

Background to the strike

The strike at the Grunwick plant which broke out in the summer of 1976 was one of the most unusual strikes ever. Although only a local dispute, it became international news. The street battles which occurred between hundreds of pickets and police were given great prominence on television. Over 550 arrests were made during the dispute – more than in any other dispute since the General Strike of 1926. The government considered the dispute so important that a special Court of Inquiry under Lord Scarman was set up, to find out the causes of the dispute and, if possible, achieve a settlement.

But the most unusual thing about the strike was that it was largely a strike of Asian workers from East Africa, most of whom were women. Of all workers, these were considered by most people to be the most docile and uncomplaining, the least likely to show any desire even to join a union, let alone to go on strike. Why then did a strike break out and why did it become so serious?

The Grunwick Processing Laboratories were founded in 1965 by three men, Anthony Grundy, George Ward and John Hickey. Grunwick was a name concocted from parts of their three names. At the time of the strike the managing director was George Ward, himself partly of Asian blood. The work of the firm was processing (developing and printing) films, at first black-and-white and later colour films. An important part of the work came by mail order. The work, which was of high standard, was done quickly and cheaply and the company was very successful. But to achieve this level of success the workers had to work hard and the wages paid were considered by some to be very low. At the time of the strike, Grunwick employed about 480 people on two sites at Cobbold Road and Chapter Road, at Willesden in north-west London.

Most of the immigrant workers at Grunwick had arrived in Britain only very recently. They had been expelled from Uganda by the notorious dictator there, Idi Amin. Their ancestors had mainly emigrated from India to East Africa in the 1890s as manual workers, but the Asians later became a successful business class in Africa and were resented by the black Africans, a fact which eventually led to the Asians being expelled.

Some of them went to India, but most came to Britain. Unlike other recent immigrants – for example, the West Indians – who had come to Britain in a period of economic expansion and low unemployment, the Ugandan Asians did not come in high expectation of discovering a better life. They came to Britain in a period of growing unemployment and economic stagnation, when prejudice against immigrants was often strong, and only as a last resort.

The East African Asian immigrants were mainly middle-class and skilled people, but on arriving in Britain they were unable to find anything other than unskilled and semi-skilled work. A survey of 1974 showed that, of all the immigrant groups, they had the highest educational qualifications, but the lowest average earnings. They felt humiliated at having to do menial work, and some of them even felt contempt for the managers who were above them, whom they believed to be less capable of doing their jobs than they themselves would have been.

The Outbreak of the Strike

The trouble at Grunwick broke out in the Mail Order Department. Of the workers here, many were women and some were students employed as temporary workers. The workers had many grievances. One of the main ones was that they were compelled to do what some of them considered excessive overtime at very short notice. The women especially were upset by this, as it forced them to neglect their children and families. Undoubtedly, discontent at Grunwick was heightened by the unusually hot weather of 1976. Conditions were difficult in the Mail Order Department where an air-

Mrs Jayaben Desai and other members of the strike committee at a press conference in August 1977.

conditioning plant had been promised, but had not arrived.

On Friday, 25 August one of the full-time workers had a dispute with the manager and decided to walk out. He was joined by three other workers, two of them part-time students.

Also that afternoon Jayaben Desai, a middle-aged woman who was to become probably the best-known of all the strikers, was involved in a dispute with the manager about compulsory overtime. She decided to walk out, and was joined by her son, Sunil.

Outside the factory the six workers met together with little idea of what to do next. They had vague ideas of joining a trade union and trying to organize a strike at Grunwick.

At 3 o'clock the next Monday afternoon about 50 workers walked out of the Chapter Road premises and marched toward the Cobbold Road laboratories. Here a certain amount of violence took place between managers and van drivers on the one hand and marchers on the other. Windows were smashed and the police were called to restore order.

By the following Friday, 137 workers out of a total work force of 480 were on strike. The strikers joined APEX, the Association for Professional, Executive, Clerical and Computer Staffs, and the union began to pay the workers strike pay.

APEX officials wrote to Hickey, the senior manager at Grunwick, asking for talks, but, following a company Board meeting, Hickey refused to meet the union, and those workers who had gone on strike were served with dismissal notices. The workers on strike said that they had been dismissed for wishing to join a union. The employers said they had been dismissed for breach of contract. George Ward said that he was not opposed to workers joining

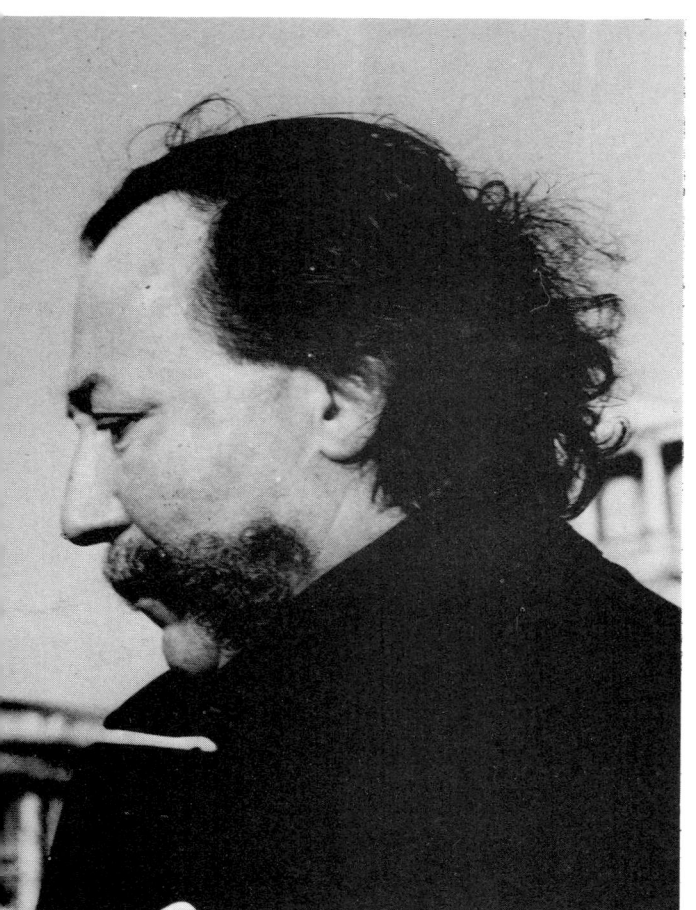
Tom Jackson.

a union, but that he refused to recognize APEX as an official negotiator on behalf of all workers at the plant.

From the very start, APEX officials threw themselves whole-heartedly into the job of supporting the strikers. Roy Grantham, the General Secretary of APEX, saw the possibilities for recruiting large numbers of workers into his union if it was seen to act decisively. But he was also convinced of the justice of the strikers' case. Very early on, he sought the help of Tom Jackson, General Secretary of the Union of Post Office Workers (UPW), Len Murray, TUC General Secretary, and of the Advisory, Conciliation and Arbitration Service (ACAS).

Strong support was also given by Len Crosby, the local official of APEX, and by the Brent Trades Council, the local branch of the TUC. A strike committee was formed and tours of local factories were organized, to get financial support for the

strikers. Marches which ended in public meetings were organized each month. A meeting also took place with the relatives of the strikers, to explain to them the purpose of the strike.

The Course of the Strike

In the first two months the strike seemed to be achieving considerable success. The company was suffering badly from the disruption of labour, especially in the Mail Order Department. Workers at the photographic company Kodak were "blacking" supplies of photographic materials destined for Grunwick. Dock workers, in Britain and on the continent, refused to handle mail going to Grunwick and post office workers at Cricklewood sorting office did the same. The strikers were confident that the company would soon seek a settlement.

Grunwick was a very prosperous company. The directors could have secured industrial peace by agreeing to the strikers' demands but they were strongly against officially recognizing the union to negotiate for the workers. George Ward said to a *Daily Telegraph* reporter:

Power rests today not with Parliament but with the trade unions . . . . The poor chap who's being exploited today is the one who's trying to run his own business.

In mid-October, Roy Grantham wrote to Albert Booth, the Secretary of State for Employment, demanding a Court of Inquiry. Booth advised APEX to refer the dispute to the Advisory, Conciliation and Arbitration Service (ACAS).

ACAS is a body set up by the government, to try to resolve disputes, but it is not responsible to the government. It has nine members. Three represent the TUC, three the CBI, and three are independent academics. ACAS can make pronouncements on what it thinks ought to be done, but it cannot enforce those decisions. Its aim is to try to persuade both sides in a dispute to behave in what it considers to be a reasonable manner.

Roy Grantham felt no enthusiasm in referring this dispute to ACAS. ACAS had tried once already, at the suggestion of APEX, to bring the two sides together, but Grunwick had refused to co-operate. There was no reason to suppose that another attempt would be any more successful, especially as the

On banner: All Trades Unions Alliance HANDS OFF BASIC RIGHTS RE INSTATE GRUNWICK STRIKERS – FOR FULL T.U. RECOGNITION THE RIGHT TO STRIKE FOR POSTMEN

TUC support.

company was now finding ways of getting round the "blacking" of mail deliveries by collecting straight from the sorting office. Moreover, ACAS would only act very slowly and delay was not on the side of the strikers.

Grantham set most store on the co-operation of the post office workers. On Friday, 28 October he persuaded the Executive Committee of the UPW (the Union of Post Office Workers) to instruct all its branches throughout the country to begin a total "blacking" of Grunwick mail. Mail would not now be handed over to the drivers of company vans.

The future now looked black for the company. Company lawyers advised that there was little that could be done legally. Ward agreed for the first time to meet ACAS. It looked as though the strikers would get their official union after all.

But, at this point, the National Association for Freedom began to play a part in the proceedings. NAFF, as it is usually called, is an organization whose expressed aim is to protect the individual from oppression by the state or other powerful organizations. It is fiercely anti-Communist and also claimed to be anti-union.

NAFF said that it was considering legal action against the postal workers. John Gorst, a member of NAFF and a Conservative MP, began to organize Conservative support for Grunwick and secured a debate in the House of Commons for Thursday, 4 November. In this debate the Minister of Employment announced that the postal workers had agreed to suspend their action against Grunwick because the company had agreed to co-operate with ACAS.

ACAS asked Grunwick for a list of all its former employees, so that they could be sent questionnaires, asking them if they wanted an official union. By Christmas Grunwick had not given ACAS the list. ACAS decided it would wait no longer and issued questionnaires on the basis of a list supplied by the union. 93 returns were made, by workers out on strike, all in favour of trade union recognition at Grunwick.

In February the company asked an independent organization, MORI, the Market Opinion Research Institute, to conduct a ballot of regular employees still at Grunwick. The result of this ballot was that 153 voted against having an officially recognized union, and 21 for.

On 10 March 1977 ACAS made its report. It recommended that the company should grant union recognition to APEX. Jim Prior, Conservative Party Shadow Minister for Employment, and known to hold conciliatory views on trades union matters, made a public statement urging the company to accept the ACAS decision.

The company did not. Instead, it served a high court writ on ACAS. It asked that the ACAS report be declared void because it was based only on the opinion of the Grunwick workers who had gone on strike.

Mass Picketing

In June 1977 strike activity reached a new pitch of intensity with the introduction of mass picketing. A mass picket is where a large group of strikers, sometimes consisting of hundreds of people, attempts to persuade workers not to enter a plant. (Pickets usually consist of only a few people.) Mass pickets had been used in a number of disputes and especially in the miners' strike of 1972. The use of mass picketing, however, was a weapon which could easily misfire because of the scenes of violence and intimidation sometimes associated with it. Any suggestion of violence or disorder on the part of the pickets would discredit the strikers' cause. The fact that the officials of APEX thought its use was justified may show that they thought it unlikely that their aims could be achieved by any other means.

Exceptional measures were considered to be justified, because the outcome of the strike was seen as important to the whole labour movement. The Strike Committee in one of its bulletins expressed it like this:

If the Strike is lost,
1 The right to organise will have been made a mockery of.
2 ACAS will have been discredited – and the Employment Protection Act.
3 Millions of unorganised workers at other Grunwicks will be discouraged from joining a union.
4 The confidence of Asian and West Indian workers in our movement will be severely discredited.
5 "Sweat Shop" employers up and down the country will take heart.

Part of the mass picket, June 1977.

Arthur Scargill.

The main purpose of the mass pickets was to draw attention to the Grunwick strike and create trade union sympathy for the strikers. Some trade unionists also hoped that the pickets would be able to physically prevent the Grunwick employees still at work from entering the factories, and so make the company give in. The Court of Inquiry was later to say, "The union, we are satisfied, had no intention of provoking violence and disorder by calling for the mass picket."

The police reaction to the mass picketing was much more positive than it had been on any previous occasion. On the very first day, 13 June, 84 pickets were arrested. The company employed a bus to drive workers still at work through the picket lines. Later, men of the Special Patrol Group, a special police force, were used to control the strikers.

On 21 June, a Labour MP was arrested on the picket line and on the 23rd Arthur Scargill (President of the Yorkshire Miners) was arrested. But, of much more importance, a police constable was injured by a flying bottle. This violent incident did the strikers' cause a great deal of harm.

The Scarman Inquiry

On 29 June the government set up a Court of Inquiry under the chairmanship of Lord Justice Scarman. APEX immediately announced that it would "co-operate with the Court of Inquiry and . . . accept its recommendations". Grunwick said it would co-operate, but did not undertake to be bound by the Inquiry's recommendations.

On 12 July, while the Scarman Inquiry was proceeding, the High Court, under Lord Chief Justice Widgery, pronounced its decision in the case brought by Grunwick against ACAS. It was in favour of ACAS. Grunwick then took the case to the Appeal Court. The Appeal Court, under the chairmanship of Lord Denning, reversed the decision. ACAS then appealed to the House of Lords.

The hearing of evidence in the Scarman Inquiry and the writing of the report took eight weeks. The report was published on 25 August. The report said the strikers had some genuine grievances, although it was critical of the postal boycott and the mass picketing.

The report recommended that the striking workers at Grunwick should be taken back into employment

by the company. On the question of union recognition, the report was not clear-cut in its recommendations. While stating that union representation was necessary at Grunwick, it left the issue to be decided by agreement between the union and the company, acting through ACAS, once the case before the House of Lords had been decided.

Many members of the Conservative Party supported George Ward in the stand he was taking. They believed that Ward was a defender of freedom against trade union oppression. Sir Keith Joseph said at a public meeting:

the unions are not automatically the oppressed. It is sometimes the employer, the job-creator, who is oppressed. Indeed it is sometimes the non-union members who are oppressed – by the unions.

Early in September the strike committee tried to persuade APEX officials to press at the TUC Congress for TUC backing for trade unionists in cutting essential services to the company. They felt this was the strongest card they had to play, but it meant breaking the law. APEX officials were unwilling to comply. Probably, it was felt that it would be very embarrassing for the Labour government if the TUC were to give such clear support for trade unionists in breaking the law. Congress passed a resolution giving full support to the strikers, but this did not commit anyone to doing anything specific.

Scenes of Violence

The strike committee turned once more to the weapon of the mass picket. On 17 October a mass picket, estimated to be 5000 strong, assembled outside Grunwick. It included a large contingent of Yorkshire miners, led by Arthur Scargill.

On Monday, 7 November a mass picket of about 8000 convergd on Grunwick. The police, said to be 4000 strong, were in position from 3.00 a.m. onwards. The day was a very violent one. 243 pickets were treated for injuries and 113 were arrested. The pickets accused the police of unnecessary violence and brutality, while much public opinion was shocked by conditions close to riot.

The End of the Strike

However, police action had been successful. The

weapon of the mass picket, so successful in the past, was seen not to be working. The forces of the law dealt severely with the arrested pickets, sentencing many of them to three months' imprisonment. Gradually, all the steam went out of the Grunwick strike movement. The public outside the trade union movement became wearied of the troubles. The strike committee found it increasingly difficult to keep up support for their cause.

On 14 December, the House of Lords announced that it upheld the decision of Lord Denning who had given judgement for Grunwick in their case against ACAS. By 1978 the strike movement was virtually at an end, though it was not until mid-July that the strike committee admitted defeat.

Conclusion

It seems at first sight surprising that, in a country which has the oldest and, many would say, one of the strongest trade union movements in the world, a strike which received such widespread support and so much publicity should have failed to win for a group of workers the right to have their trade union recognized. Why was George Ward able to defy successfully the combined power of the TUC, the findings of the Scarman Inquiry and the bulk of left-wing political opinion in the country?

Some people believe that the TUC was itself mainly to blame. In many European countries George Ward would have been compelled by law to recognize APEX. It has been argued that Britain should have something like the American system, where an employer is compelled by law to recognize a union which has majority support among the workers and also to bargain in good faith with that union – however, this would not have resulted in union recognition at Grunwick where a majority was not in favour. The TUC has little liking for such a system. It is very difficult to prove whether or not an employer is indeed bargaining in good faith, and disputes can go on almost endlessly about this. The TUC also has little faith in British courts. It prefers the present system where trade union powers are often wider than in America, though possibly less secure.

The main reason for the outcome at Grunwick was, however, the attitude of the Labour government then nearing the end of its term of office. Naturally, it was anxious to be re-elected at the next election. It believed that, if the public thought it was too left-wing and "soft" on law and order, this would be damaging to its chances. That is probably why, under a Labour Home Secretary, police arrested 550 pickets and use was made of the Special Patrol Group against strikers and demonstrators. Almost certainly, the Labour government, if it had really wished to, could have ensured the success of the strike. The failure of the strike gave great heart to those on the right wing who are hostile to trade union powers.

TRADE UNIONS ABROAD

Trade unionism has developed very differently in different countries, and the British pattern of trade unionism is only one among many. We would naturally expect the trade union scene to be different in countries which have different histories and circumstances from Britain's. But even in countries which are English-speaking and where early trade unionism came under British influence, trade union development has been dissimilar.

Australian Unions

One country where British influence has been important is Australia.

Numerically, the Australian unions are strong. About 53% of all Australian workers belong to unions. This compares closely with about 50% in Britain. British-style craft unions were taken to Australia by British immigrants in the nineteenth century and the variety of types of union is as great as in Britain.

A confederation of manual workers' trade unions, the ACTU, was formed in the inter-war years. (There are several separate white-collar federations.) The ACTU prepares claims on pay and other matters for presentation to the federal government authorities, but most of the actual settlements are not made for one type of work nation-wide, but at the level of the individual states. The federation has only sometimes organized the unions in strike activity.

Population in Australia is concentrated in the capital cities of the six states. Because of this, the state branch is very important in most Australian unions. The branch organization appoints its own officers, and many unions at national level are little more than committees of state branch representatives. It is at state branch level that competition takes place for control of the union. Australian unions are often split deeply along political lines, between Communists, Labour, and the Conservative groups, including the Catholics. Competition for power is often fierce.

As in Britain, shop stewards and shop steward committees have become more important recently, but they have not as yet acquired the power they have in Britain. This is probably because both employers and full-time trade union officials are hostile to shop stewards. The employers see them as extremist and the union officials think them a challenge to their own power.

Australia has a distinctive method of regulating industrial relations. If employers and unions fail to agree on union wage claims, the dispute is settled by a special arbitration court set up by the government. The decisions of the court are binding on both parties for the period of the agreement.

This would seem at first sight to be an ideal way of ensuring industrial peace, but, in fact, Australian industrial relations are not particularly harmonious. Production time lost through strikes is second only to that in the USA, even though certain kinds of strikes are illegal in all states, and all strikes are illegal in Western Australia.

In general, the unions have welcomed the work of the arbitration courts. The government helped establish the unions and later protected them. But recently, governments have come to believe that union power needs curbing and they have the power to do that. The industrial courts can interpret and alter union rules and supervise union ballots.

United States Unions

Trade unionism began early in the United States with the setting up of craft unions on the British model. But, for a long time, unions did not spread widely. This was largely because of the numbers of immigrants who poured into the country during the nineteenth and early twentieth centuries. These immigrants, often poor and desperate for jobs, were willing to work for long hours and low wages, and unwilling to risk antagonizing their employees by joining unions.

The early craft unions formed a confederation of unions called the American Federation of Labour

Wilbur Hobby, President of the North Carolina State AFL-CIO.

(AFL). The unions, usually industrial unions, which came into existence later, came together in the Congress of Industrial Organizations (CIO). Later, the two federations joined to form the AFL-CIO.

The AFL-CIO is not a very powerful federation. This is partly because the two largest unions in the United States are not members. The Auto Workers withdrew from the federation, and the Teamsters' union, which began as a union of lorry drivers and is now a general union containing workers from many industries and occupations, was expelled for corruption. But the AFL-CIO has considerable influence on the international trade union movement. This is because, like many American institutions, it is extremely wealthy.

Most wage bargaining in the USA is conducted at company or plant level. Once negotiations have been concluded, both sides of industry are legally bound to honour their side of the bargain for the period for which the agreement is to run – usually two or three years. Strikes during this time are illegal. A number of people in Britain would like to see this system adopted in this country. They think that it would help to cut down the number of strikes. This is in spite of the fact that more time is lost annually by strikes in the USA than in any other major industrial country.

Only a small proportion of American workers are union members. This is partly because Americans generally are supporters of individual economic enterprise. Trade unions do not seem to fit easily into the American way of life. Employers are sometimes hostile to trade unionism. Many American workers, especially white collar workers, feel that they have more to lose, by angering the boss, than they have to gain from union membership. It was not until 1962, under President Kennedy, that any form of wage bargaining was allowed for public sector workers. Previously, their wages and salaries were simply fixed by government and they were not allowed to strike.

America is often thought of as the home of the great trade union "boss", a bullying and often corrupt trade union dictator. There have been a number of trade union leaders who have more or less fitted this description. Some have even been proved to have had connections with the Mafia. But their power has rarely been absolute. Sooner or later, ways have been found of removing them from office. In fact, in many unions, the officials at state branch level are more powerful than the national officers.

There is often bitter fighting for power inside the unions, but this is not usually, as in most other countries, on political lines. It is usually between individual leaders and their followers. This is because the so-called "spoils system", which operates in American government, also operates in a large number of unions. The leader who has been appointed to high office, whether in government or union, begins his term of office by sacking the existing officials and replacing them with his friends and supporters. Obviously, such a system leads rather easily to corruption.

French Unions
French trade unionism follows a distinctive pattern. Up until 1914 it was dominated by the ideas of Syndicalism, a strong movement in France. It aimed at seizing political power for the workers by a series of strikes. It was thought that, once the workers had seized power, the parliament and government would be replaced by government through trade unions. Each union would represent the workers of a particular industry.

Because of these beliefs, early French trade unionists did not aim for the improvement of workers' pay and conditions through negotiation with employers. To have done this would have been to accept the rightness and the probable permanence of the capitalist system. The real aim of the unions was to seize political power by strike action. They realized that this might not be possible for some time. In the meantime, concessions could be won from the employers by strikes and threat of strikes.

When Syndicalist influences waned, the importance of the Communists in the French trade unions grew. The Communists have taken over many of the ideas of the Syndicalists. Not nearly as much effort has been made in France towards building up a system of wage bargaining as in other countries.

By 1914 a number of unions existed, most of them industrial unions, which were formed together into a Communist federation, the CGT. In 1945 a Catholic trade union movement, the CFTC, came into existence and in 1947 an anti-Communist minority pulled out of the CGT, to form the CGT-FO. Later, a left-wing but non-Communist movement, the CFTD, split itself from the Catholic movement. The picture is certainly very complicated.

The Communist CGT is by far the strongest of these federations, but, even so, it has only a half of the total union membership. In most other countries, one confederation is clearly stronger than all its rivals put together. Most French workers have the choice of three or four unions, split on political or religious grounds. Strictly speaking, what we have called the confederations are really the unions, each one divided into a number of industrial sections. If a French worker is asked what union he belongs to, he will say the CGT or the CFDT, not the Engineers or the Miners.

Trade union membership in France is low, about 25%. This is largely because French employers have fought hard and generally successfully to resist the spread of trade unionism. Many French firms are still family businesses. The employer often sees himself as "le patron", the father, who keeps all the power in his own hands and treats his workers as his children.

Unions have the legal right to exist and organize in every workplace. Union officials have the right to collect subscriptions, call meetings, have time off to do their work, and arrange meetings with management. But the management are not compelled to bargain with the unions. Management must register the workers' grievances, but do not need to do anything about them.

Strikes are not illegal in France. They can be called even by the workplace trade union officials. The unions believe in the use of the strike weapon and employers do not go out of their way to avoid strikes. Even so, the loss of time through strikes in France is nowhere nearly so great as in America.

There were many strikes in the period 1947-51. This was because the Communist party had just left the post-war coalition government and called on the CGT to organize a series of political strikes. Eventually, most workers became tired of strikes, membership of trade unions decreased, and the CGT was forced into more moderate policies.

France soon entered a period of economic growth, at a rate almost equalling that of West Germany. Increased economic growth led to increased wages and industrial harmony. The government has been able to manage without resorting to an incomes policy. But it has held back pay increases in the nationalized industries, partly in order to set an example to the private sector of industry, and the result has been a number of major strikes.

West German Unions

By 1914 trade unions of many different kinds were strongly established in Germany. With the coming to power of the dictator Hitler in 1933, trade unions were abolished. At the end of the Second World War in 1945, there was therefore an opportunity to create a completely new trade union structure in the new West German state. The pattern chosen was industrial unionism. Sixteen unions were created, each covering an industry or group of industries. It has been described by Hugh Clegg, Professor of Industrial Relations at Warwick University, as the "neatest and most simplified industrial plan that has ever been created". It is in sharp contrast to the complicated picture presented by the British trade union scene. Ironically, British trade union leaders played an important part in creating it.

The main confederation of trade unions is the DGB (Deutsche Gewerkschaftsbund). It plays no part in wage negotiations, but it has a wide range of other activities, including housing, banking and supplying advice and information services to member unions.

Bargaining is supposed to be at regional level, but in many industries agreements covering the whole country are signed by union and employers, which serve as a guide for regional settlements. The employers' organizations discipline their individual member companies into accepting the national settlements, and the unions pride themselves on honouring their agreements.

Germany has been entirely free of major strikes and German industrial relations are the envy of most other countries. One possible explanation is that German workers are more disciplined and responsible than workers elsewhere. This is an argument often heard in Britain. But there are a number of other factors to be taken into account. Germany's simplified system of union organization, and the major role played by workers' councils and worker managers in many industries, giving workers a greater say in how industry is run are probably very important.

But, most important of all is Germany's "economic miracle". For many years, Germany has enjoyed economic prosperity. Neither unions nor employers have wanted to do anything to endanger this. It remains to be seen whether relations will be so easy, now that Germany has run into economic difficulties.

Most unions before Hitler's time were affiliated to the Social Democratic Party, but after the war it was decided that the unions would not be linked to any of the political parties, because this might divide the union movement. However, most German trade unionists have socialist beliefs, and relations between the unions and the Social Democratic Party are very close.

Swedish Unions

Trade unions, especially those for manual workers, were well-established in Sweden before the end of the nineteenth century and grew rapidly in the early years of this century. In 1912 the main union federation, the LO (Landsorganisationen i Sverige), accepted the principle of industrial unionism. Since then, it has consistently tried to reduce the number of trade unions by amalgamations. At present, most unions, but not all, are industrial unions.

In 1936 a law was passed compelling employers to recognize trade unions. This was aimed especially at increasing the spread of white collar unions. The result has been that 71% of white collar workers in the public sector are union members, compared with 27% in Britain and only 9% in the USA. Trade unions are respected in Sweden and are accepted ungrudgingly by employers. Sweden has by far the highest percentage of its workforce in unions, 87%.

Besides the powerful LO, there is a smaller federation of white collar unions, the TCO. Because the LO has remained a federation of manual workers' unions, it has abided consistently by its early belief in equality. It is far less concerned than trade union movements in other countries with maintaining a system of higher pay for more highly skilled workers, and more concerned with securing high basic rates of pay for all workers.

Swedish unions are well-organized and pursue long-term policies. Union leaders are respected and strongly supported by rank and file members. There seems to be very little bickering in the unions. They are powerful and effective.

The annual conference, composed of elected delegates, is the supreme authority in the union. It elects the executive bodies and the full-time officers. Union branches have recently been reduced in number and made larger, so that they can employ more paid officers. The branches are kept very firmly under the control of the central headquarters. The LO uses its influence to increase the power of the chief union officer within the union whenever possible.

Industrial bargaining takes place at industry level, but settlements are now usually guided by general agreements which are negotiated first between the LO and the SAF (the employers' confederation).

The strength and unity of the LO are matched by those of the long-established SAF. The SAF insists on bargaining centrally for each industry as a whole, and is very strong in insisting that none of its member companies makes separate wage settlements with workers. This is in great contrast with Great Britain where the CBI, a relatively recent creation, has very little control over its member companies. Because wage bargaining is organized centrally in Sweden, the unions have to be organized centrally. There is no reason why a strong shop steward movement should develop.

The LO is probably stronger than the union federation of any other country. This is partly because it has a close relationship with the Social Democratic Party which held office almost continuously for over forty years. The Social Democrats have consistently pursued social and economic policies which the unions like. In return, the unions have behaved responsibly. There have been few strikes. Sweden has had fewer strikes than any country except West Germany. As in that country, industrial relations have been helped by the long period of economic prosperity and the high standard of living. But credit must also be given to the restraint, common-sense and desire for social consensus which seems to prevail in Sweden.

WORKERS' PARTICIPATION AND THE UNIONS

Problems of Industrial Work

Many people in industrialized societies today are deeply dissatisfied with their work. Increased use of machinery has almost completely eliminated the need for workers to do long hours of heavy physical labour, but modern workers do not necessarily find their now lighter work attractive. Many complain that it is boring and repetitive. Work is seen by many workers primarily not as an end in itself, but as a way of getting money with which to satisfy leisure-time needs. The hours spent outside work are seen by the worker as his real life. The hours spent at work have to be got through somehow.

And yet there is a strong belief at the back of most people's minds that work is indispensable for life. Few people want to be unemployed. Work ought to be more than a source of wages, people feel. It ought to be meaningful, satisfying, enjoyable.

Modern conditions of work began with the industrial revolution. Adam Smith, the famous eighteenth-century political economist, observed the methods of working in a pin factory of his day. The process of making a pin, at first sight a very simple article, was divided into no fewer than 18 distinct operations, each one carried out by separate groups of workers. He calculated that, in this way, the workers produced 240 times as many pins as they could have done if each man had tried to produce an entire pin on his own.

He was full of admiration for the efficient and economical way in which the work was done. But he did say:

> The man whose life is spent in performing a few simple operations . . . has no occasion to exert his understanding or to exercise his invention in finding out expedients for removing difficulties which never occur . . . and generally becomes as stupid and ignorant as it is possible for a human being to become.

As the nineteenth century progressed, more and more workers found that their lives were dominated by the tyranny of the machine. But towards the end of the century another tyranny was added, that of Scientific Management.

Scientific Management

It all began with an American, Frederick W. Taylor. He was a steel worker who rose to be chief engineer of a Philadelphia steel company.

He believed that the men employed by the company did not work nearly as hard as they could. Management had offered the workers higher wages

Adam Smith.

and promises of promotion to encourage higher productivity, but even this had little effect.

Taylor came to the conclusion that each job had a single best way of being done. This could be discovered scientifically and enforced. He carefully watched men doing a job. He decided which of the moves they made were really necessary and he made the men cut out all useless movements. This was the origin of "time and motion study", which has by now been applied all over the world.

Taylor conducted an experiment in loading pig iron. The average rate at the time was 12½ tons per day per man, which he believed was too low. Taylor picked out what he considered a rather unintelligent worker and promised him large bonus payments if he would do exactly as he was told. His instructions were:

> You will do exactly as this man [pointing to the foreman] tells you tomorrow, from morning till night. When he tells you to pick up a pig [a bar of iron], you pick it up and you walk, and when he tells you to sit down and rest, you sit down. You do that straight through the day and no talk back. Do you understand that? When this man tells you to walk, you walk; when he tells you to sit down, you sit down and you don't talk back to him.

The man did as he was told and the result was that he moved 47½ tons in the day.

Taylor realized that only mentally sluggish people would put up with working in this way. The more alert workers would soon find the work too monotonous. It was essential therefore, he believed, that the workers should be disciplined rigidly. He said:

> It is only through *enforced* standardisation of methods, *enforced* adoption of the best implements and working conditions, and *enforced* co-operation that the faster work can be assured. And the duty of enforcing rests with management alone.

The worker, Taylor believed, had to work, not think:

> All possible brain work should be removed from the shop, and centred in the planning or lay-out department. The time during which the man stops

to think is part of the time that he is not productive.

The new kind of organization would make work less attractive, but this could be overcome by paying higher wages from the profits of increased efficiency.

Scientific Management spread rapidly and is now often applied to all sorts of jobs. Time and motion experts with their clip-boards and stop-watches are a familiar sight in many large factories and offices.

The Workers' Reaction

Some managers may have been enthusiastic about the new methods of production, but the workers have been much less so. Often, they have been made to feel powerless in a meaningless and boring job.

Many examples can be cited of workers whose task, day after day, is so simple and so repetitious that it is hard to understand how anyone can put up with it. One often-quoted example of such work is that in car assembly plants. It was brilliantly portrayed in a famous Charlie Chaplin film, *Modern Times*.

One worker who spoke to an interviewer had the job of putting bolts into one particular hole in car bodies. They were delivered to him in barrels of 10,000. He said:

> When you've used them all up you're given another barrel and so on and so on. It's not a matter of pace. It's the monotony. It's not good for you to get so bored. I do the same thing day after day; it's just an ever-lasting grind.

Scientific Management principles have been applied to office work as well as to manual work. The dissatisfaction of office workers has grown because of this and has spread to management itself. An American Management Association report spoke of "increasing management discontent" due to the "highly bureaucratic and authoritarian structures of modern industrial and commercial concerns. Decision-making has become the work of only a few at the very top of each enterprise."

This change has come at a time when rising standards of education make for greater discontent. More educated people usually need and expect to find responsibility and satisfaction in work.

Many people today, including managers, recognize the need to change the nature of work if

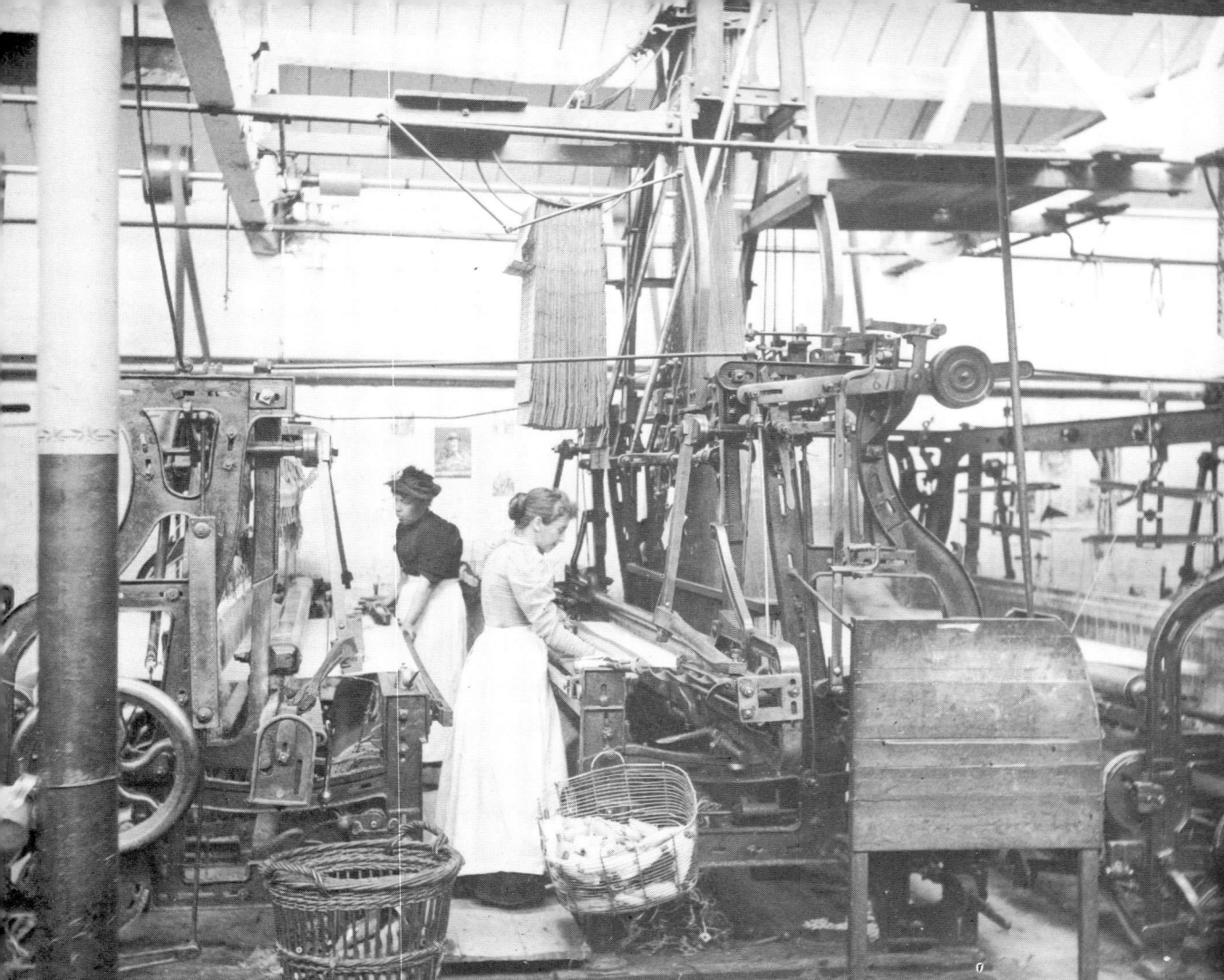

The "tyranny of the machine". (Blanket mill, c.1900.)

this is at all possible. If work is too boring, monotonous and repetitive, the solution seems to be to put the different parts of the job together again to provide more "whole work". If work is too authoritarian and gives the worker no scope for decision-making, then the solution seems to be to make it more democratic, to give the worker more chance to use his intelligence and to take on responsibility.

G.D.H. Cole, Marx and Lenin

Ideas of this kind are not new. As early as the inter-war period an English socialist thinker, G.D.H. Cole, originator of theories which he called "Guild Socialism", questioned why so much stress was often placed on political democracy and so little on industrial democracy. He attacked both capitalist bureaucratic control and what he called collectivist (socialist or Communist) bureaucratic control. The workers, he believed, must be given:

> responsibility and control, in short, freedom to express their personality in their work . . . . Political democracy must be complemented by democracy in the workshop.

One man who was aware of the difficulties faced by the workers in modern industry, even before the advent of Taylor's Scientific Management, was the social theorist and Communist, Karl Marx. He called the problem "work alienation" and wrote at considerable length about it:

The production line at Toshiba's Fukaya works in Japan, which turns out 25,000 colour television sets a month. ►

60

A scene from *Modern Times*.

George Douglas Howard Cole.

Alienation exists when workers are unable to control their immediate work processes, to develop a sense of purpose and function which connects their jobs to the over-all organization of production . . . and when they fail to become involved in the activity of work as a mode of personal self-expression.

In 1917, when Lenin and the Communists seized power in Russia, they were acting on and testing Marx's theories. Lenin's slogan was "All power to the Workers' and Soldiers' Soviets" (Soviets were workers' councils) and industries were initially placed under the workers' control. It was a time of civil war and upheaval in Russia and it is impossible to say how successful the experiment was. At the end of about a year, however, workers' control was replaced by "Workers' Management" which was something different. It was a highly disciplined system of management by top party officials and managers.

Lenin had a great admiration for the achievements of Western industrialism, and even for the theories of Scientific Management. He said:

We must organize in Russia the study and teaching

of the Taylor system and systematically try it ou and adapt it to our own needs.

A management class soon developed in Russia as i the West, and work there became highly disciplined The Russian Labour Law of 1970 states that:

it is the duty of the factory workers and offic employees to work honestly and conscientiously to observe labour discipline, to carry out th orders of the administration promptly an accurately, to raise productivity, to improve th quality of the products, observe the requirement of the production techniques . . . .

Nor did the fact that the means of production wer now officially owned by the workers, or by the stat which acted in their name, necessarily make th workers more content than under capitalism Experience seems to show that work alienation is jus as widespread in the Communist world as in th capitalist.

Workers' Councils

Workers' councils (usually called Joint Consultativ Committees in Britain) were set up in Norway Sweden, France, Holland and West Germany afte the Second World War. Their role is purel consultative, enabling workers to make suggestion to managers, who still make the decisions.

They are usually independent of the unions an represent all workers, whether union members c not, concerning themselves more with wor conditions than with the wage matters which usuall dominate union negotiation. Of course, unio officials are often active in these councils, so th distinction between the two organizations may b stronger in theory than in practice.

Workers' councils have not had a great impac Some workers believe that they are there to give ther a "feeling" of participation rather than any rea power. In Sweden, it has been said, they give scop "for a full and frank exchange of views", but hav little influence on management policy. In France, th employers regard workers' councils as a threat t their powers and tend not to co-operate with them.

Councils have probably achieved their greates success in West Germany. They first developed ther during the short-lived Weimar Republic from 192

The opening of the 1982 Congress of the Soviet trade unions.

Workers at a watch factory in the Soviet Union. A round of keep-fit exercises at 11 in the morning is compulsory in all offices and factories. ▼

The laundry room, Kerem Shalom Kibbutz.

to 1933. When they were re-established after the period of Hitler's rule, careful, but largely unsuccessful, precautions were taken to limit trade union influence in them. But, probably, they owe what strength they have to union participation and to their important part in the wider system of worker-management consultation in West German industry.

After the industrial troubles of 1956, workers' councils were established in Communist Poland. They had strong support from workers, but very little support from the Communist-controlled trade unions. Once the government felt more secure again, they were abolished. Possibly, if the Solidarity Free Trade Union movement of the early 1980s had not been forcibly ended by the imposition of military government, Poland's workers' councils would have become a permanent feature of the country's industrial life.

The Kibbutzim of Israel

An interesting experiment in workers' democracy or workers' participation has been made in Israel. The Israeli kibbutzim are now world-famous and many students and young people from the West go each year to work on them.

The first kibbutz was established in 1900. Now there are about 230, with 90,000 members. They are all owned and operated by the members themselves.

At the time of their formation, Jews in Europe, where the majority of Jews then lived, were barred from working in agriculture. On reaching Israel, some of the them wanted to break away from their traditional lives in commerce and cities, believing in the moral value of manual work, especially in agriculture.

The early kibbutz members were the pioneering élite of the new nation of Israel. Since then they have always made an important contribution to the country's life. In this they are unlike groups in other countries who live in self-sufficient communities, who have tended to become isolated from life outside.

The organization of the kibbutz is thoroughly democratic. Members rotate between different jobs. They do not receive a high salary. Each person or family group is simply given enough money to satisfy basic needs, such as food, education and housing. The foreman is paid no more than the ordinary worker. Older workers are given lighter work, but do not suffer a reduction in wages. There is no real private property, and, something that has aroused great controversy outside the kibbutz, children are brought up by the community as a whole.

From a commercial point of view, at least, the experiment has worked very well. Despite the respect for manual labour, modern scientific methods of

Harvesting grapefruit on the kibbutz.

agriculture have been eagerly adopted. Agriculture has prospered.

Increased mechanization of agriculture led to some members having no work. Many kibbutzim therefore began to set up light industries, many of them closely connected with agriculture, to absorb their surplus labour.

In some cases, those industries have been so successful that the kibbutz has had to take on hired workers from outside. Usually, this has led to severe problems. It has been difficult to lead the new workers to accept the spirit of the kibbutz. As commercial undertakings have grown, democratic management has often tended to be replaced by bureaucratic and authoritarian organization.

The kibbutzim have undoubtedly proved that industrial democracy can work and be commercially efficient and successful. But they probably have limited value as a model to be copied elsewhere. This is because of the special conditions of Israeli society and social ideals in which they operate.

Workers' Democracy in Yugoslavia

In 1945, after the war of liberation against the Germans, the Communist state of Yugoslavia was set up. All industry came into state ownership and industrial control was in the hands of the central government. In the chaotic economic conditions of the time this seemed the only possible course of action.

At first, there was a continuation of the war-time spirit and tremendous enthusiasm among the people to build up shattered industries. But gradually this enthusiasm was stifled by bureaucratic control from the top.

In 1948 affairs in Yugoslavia took a dramatic change in direction. Tito, the Yugoslav president, quarrelled with the Soviet dictator Stalin, and Yugoslavia was expelled from the Cominform, the international organization of Communist states dominated by the Soviet Union.

The Yugoslav leaders did not wish to renounce their Communism, but they did want to be independent of Moscow. They did not want to set up an industrial system on the Western capitalist model, as they believed this was a system of exploitation. But, on the other hand, they wanted to break away from the Soviet pattern where all economic life was controlled by the central state organization.

The writings of Karl Marx, the inspirer of Communism, were re-examined and evidence found to support the decentralization of industry. A certain amount of control over industry was transferred from the central state authority to the six regional republics and to the town councils. Workers' councils were set up in factories and a law was passed setting up "management by collectives". Ownership of economic enterprises was officially said to belong not to the state or the workers, but to society as a whole.

The task of re-organization and reconstruction facing Yugoslavia after the war was enormous. 10% of the population had been killed in the war. 75% of the population were still employed in agriculture. The industries which had existed before the war had been largely foreign-owned. As late as 1961, 25% of the population were illiterate. Within the country there were many divisions between different ethnic, religious and cultural groups. There were even two different alphabets in use. However, in spite of all this, much progress has been made.

Each factory, office or farm has a workers' council which has to approve all management decisions, such as appointments, salary scales, dismissals, investment and long-term policy. Members of the council are elected for two years and receive no additional pay, continuing with their ordinary jobs. At first, the managers were appointed by the town councils, but now they are elected by the workers' council.

In 1961 economic units (smaller groups in larger companies) were set up. This was done to involve more workers in policy making and bring them closer to the centre of power in the company. A large company may have as many as ten economic units.

A general manager commenting on his position had this to say:

I don't make decisions – I only make suggestions to the workers' council. Most of the time they are accepted. But they have to be explained in great detail so that the workers can understand them. If the council decides differently and I don't accept their decision they can make me resign.

A certain proportion of company profits have to be used as the government thinks fit. Help is given to depressed areas, for instance. But what is left over is allocated as the workers' council wants, and the council has control over wages and salaries. Usually, managers are paid about four or five times the wage of the lowest-paid workers. Experience shows that the proportion of profits given to wages as against investment has not been excessive.

Many studies have been made of the Yugoslavian system, arriving at very different conclusions. But most judgments seem quite favourable. Relations between workers and management seem better than in most other countries.

At first, only a few workers really got involved in the system, but, over the years, workers' involvement has increased enormously. This is probably due to increased education and literacy.

The system is often criticized because it takes too much power away from management and prevents decisive action. On the other hand it may be argued that it prevents management behaving dictatorially and irresponsibly. The enterprises with the most active councils are usually the most successful. It may be that this is because an active council keeps management on its toes.

The newspaper, the *Economist*, had this to say:

One thing is clear, workers' self-management cannot be pronounced to be an economic failure, as its critics in communist countries shrilly insist . . . certainly from the workers' angle it is preferable to a centralised system of state management.

In 1958 there was considerable industrial unrest in Yugoslavia and widespread strikes, whose legality under the Constitution was disputed. Eventually, strikes were made legal. A difficult situation had existed in the country. Workers were free to speak their mind on matters affecting their working lives, but in political matters they were expected to obey Communist Party orders without question. Tito resolved the problem by granting greater political freedom.

The better work atmosphere in Yugoslav factories which many observers believe now exists may well be due to the good communications which exist between workforce and management. The workers have better information on the company they work for, its difficulties, prospects and achievements, than do workers in many other countries.

A French observer of the Yugoslav system comments:

It has in only fifteen years managed to bring about the basic industrialization of the country which it took us more than a century to achieve, and despite some abuses Yugoslavia attained this result in a much more humane fashion.

Co-determination in West Germany

At the end of the Second World War, defeated by the victorious Allied powers, Germany was divided into zones of occupation. The Ruhr, the main area of Germany's iron and steel industries, was inside the British zone. The German Labour movement suggested that workers should be given a share in the management of the factories. This scheme, usually known as co-determination (*Mitbestimmung*), would act as a check on management. The British Labour government which exercised great influence until West Germany became fully independent agreed with the suggestion.

In each iron and steel company, supervisory boards were set up on which workers and shareholders were equally represented. The idea was later extended to all large companies outside the iron and steel industry. Here, workers formed a third of the directors on supervisory boards. The supervisory boards appoint the managers, but have no control over day-to-day decisions of the managerial board.

Critics of the system argue that worker directors have in fact little real power. Power really lies with the managerial board, they say. But the changes have ensured that workers' views and interests are taken into account in matters such as cutbacks in jobs and changes in technology, and tension within the workplace has probably been lessened.

Social Scientists in the USA

In the USA social scientists have studied the problems of industrial production in great detail. Many of them have come to be critical of the ideas of Scientific Management.

Modern industry and commerce, these critics say, satisfy the more basic needs of the worker – for security and freedom from hunger – but not his higher needs for satisfaction and achievement. Only when these needs are met, will the worker be really happy and work to his full capacity.

Douglas McGregor, a social scientist, asserts that there are two basically different approaches possible to management. The traditional approach he labels the X theory of management. According to this theory, men have a built-in dislike of work. Therefore, if workers are to work hard, they must be coerced, directed and even punished.

According to the opposing theory of management, the Y theory, work is as natural as play or rest. Workers will, if allowed to, take on responsibility, exercise self-control and are capable of showing imagination, creativity and ingenuity.

McGregor believes that the authoritarian X approach is bad for the workers and for the company. It wastes the most valuable asset a company has, the intelligence and commitment of its employees. No company, he says, would ever dream of wasting its resources of machinery, plant and computers in a similar way.

In contrast, he says, the Y approach is good for both workers and company. Indeed, it seeks to harmonize the goals of both, and so the organization is altered to fit the needs of the individuals in it, rather than the reverse. The new ideas have been tried out by a number of American businessmen.

But many managers believe that they have the right and ability to manage, and that decision-making will be weakened if more people become involved. Therefore, they oppose the Y theory of management.

Taylor and the believers in Scientific Management tried to make work as simple and repetitive as possible. Those who believe in the Y theory are trying to do exactly the opposite. They lay stress on the need to make work more varied, more demanding, more responsible. Workers are encouraged to learn a variety of jobs by moving from job to job, and this is brought about by bonus payments and earlier promotion.

Frederick Hertzberg is probably the best-known work social scientist in the US, who has worked to spread the new ideas of management. Although he seeks to give workers more responsibility, he is not opposed to managers being the leaders. He believes that managers must decide what changes are to be made, and he is opposed to the idea of group discussion.

Robert Likert, Director of the Institute of Social Research at Michigan University, has gone much further. He believes that the workers themselves should work out necessary changes, set their own targets, decide on work methods and even on budgets. In effect, he believes that they should take over much of the work of management.

These participative methods are the real heart of industrial democracy. It is perhaps strange that in countries such as the US and Britain people pride themselves on their political democracy but show little interest in industrial democracy. Yet it is argued by some people that real political democracy is impossible in a country which does not have industrial democracy also.

Workers' participation in the USA

Workers' participation has been tried out in a number of companies in the USA with great success. Changes made have included the replacement of payment by results with a system of salary grades, the removal of time clocks, the handing over of quality checking from inspectors to the production workers themselves, and workers being allowed to maintain and repair the machines they operate.

One manager who was involved commented:

> It proves two things: first, people are basically honest; second, they really want to do as good a job as possible.

One important firm which believes in workers' participation is the electronics giant, Texas Instruments. In 1960 it had sales of over 200 million dollars and was the world's largest manufacturer of semi-conductors. But it was faced by ever-increasing competition and decided not to rest on its laurels.

The aim was that "every person" should be "a manager". Every worker was given as much responsibility as he could cope with. The old distinctions of better office furnishings for managers, and executive car parks, dining rooms and lavatories were done away with. Everyone was encouraged to call each other by Christian names. The experience of this firm was said to demonstrate "the wastefulness of bureaucracy and the advantages of democracy".

A small new electronics firm in New Jersey, Cosning Glass, decided to try out the new methods. Emphasis was placed on making jobs more challenging and setting up independent work groups. In one department the assembly line was scrapped and each person assembled the whole product. "Now it's my hot-plate" said one girl machine operator.

Absenteeism dropped from 8% to 1% of all workers in six months. Rejected products dropped from 23% to 1% of all products, and productivity rose by 47%.

Proctor and Gamble, which with Lever Brothers dominates the soap and washing-powder market in Britain and is the 21st largest company in the US, has experimented widely with industrial democracy. Company policy is to encourage workers to use their full potential to tackle difficult jobs. Conference rooms have been built next to work areas, to make discussion easier. "Class distinctions" have been reduced. There are no time clocks. Everyone is paid a salary worked out by open discussion, and agreed by everyone and known to everyone. The new methods have met with success even in company plants which previously had been a byword for failure.

New and freer approaches to management have often been successful in large and small companies alike in the USA, the original home of Taylorism. But, even so, the American business world as a whole remains unconvinced that the new ideas are the best way of achieving company goals.

Experiments with Participation in Britain

Among the earliest believers in new approaches to management in industry were the social scientists of the Tavistock Institute of Human Relations in London. They conducted a number of research projects, including one with Glacier Metal, a London-based company making industrial bearings.

Even before the research project began, the management was working towards new methods. They had instituted paid leave for all employees and had abolished time clocks. These changes had not led to increased absenteeism or unpunctuality. A workers' council had also been set up for the discussion of problems, but this had not been very successful.

At the suggestion of the research workers, this council was expanded to include office workers. Most important of all, it was given the power to make decisions which the management agreed to carry out. Managers found that, as a result of these changes, their own effectiveness was increased, not diminished.

The Tavistock findings were that organizations were most efficient if the work force was divided into small work groups run on democratic lines, with as much independence as possible.

The Institute was given a chance to try out an experiment in the coal industry. The nationalization of the coal industry which took place after the Second World War had been expected to produce an improvement in worker-management relations, but this had not happened. Nor had the introduction of highly mechanized processes produced the expected gains in productivity.

The traditional method of cutting coal had been for teams of six men working in three shifts to tackle a coal face 6 to 11 yards long. Payment was made according to the productivity of the group.

This method was changed after nationalization to the long-wall method. A team of forty men working in three shifts and using complex machinery tackled a coal face 80 to 100 yards long. In accordance with the ideas of Scientific Management, the work was broken up into as many separate tasks as possible. As far as possible, each man did only one job the whole time. The result was that the men felt bored and not involved in their work.

The Tavistock experiment was to return towards the earlier system. Each group of miners tackled the entire business of coal-cutting. Each miner was encouraged to do several jobs and to change jobs frequently. A productivity payment was made to each group on the basis of its performance.

The productivity of a group of miners working on the long-wall method was compared with that of a group working according to the Tavistock recommendations. The first group was judged to have reached 78% of its maximum possible output and the second group 95%. Also, the morale of the second group improved. Sickness and absenteeism decreased dramatically and there was little or no need for their work to be supervised.

The Tavistock findings were not generally welcomed by British management and the Coal Board did not introduce the new system of working. It seems as though British society is too conservative for these ideas to gain easy acceptance. Most managers, like many trade unionists, are locked in ideas of "them" and "us" and believe in the inevitability of industrial conflict.

At least until recently, the trade unions in Britain have been suspicious of workers becoming involved in management. But in 1966 Jack Jones, leader of the Transport and General Workers' Union, expressed his belief in it. He saw management as "lazy and inept" and in need of reform. In 1967 the Labour Party adopted a resolution favouring industrial democracy, but very little action has resulted from it.

Anthony Wedgwood Benn is one of the Labour leaders who has been strong in his championing of industrial democracy. He says:

> The man who has to actually do a job of work on the factory floor, or in a shop or office, is the best person to know how his or her work ought to be organized. There is nothing that creates more ill-will in industry than when people are denied the elementary authority to plan and guide the work they are qualified to do . . . . Workers are consistently underestimated and their intelligence insulted.

In the late 1970s a committee of enquiry, under the chairmanship of Alan Bullock, the Oxford historian, produced a report on industrial democracy, generally known as the Bullock Report. It wished to see industrial democracy extended to all sizeable companies in Britain. But the trade union movement, managers and the government were not enthusiastic and little progress was made.

In the early 1980s, with an economic recession, high unemployment and a Conservative government in power, the idea of industrial democracy has fallen into the background. Although most of the political parties pay lip service to industrial democracy, little is likely to be done in the next few years.

Conclusion

It has been shown by examples from many countries that industrial democracy and participation can be successful in increasing both profits and workers' satisfaction. However, more industrial democracy is still opposed by some. There are several reasons for this. One is the fact that companies are usually owned by a group of shareholders, and it is felt that to make workers responsible for running the company would interfere with the right of the people who actually own the company to run it. Another reason is that most managers oppose such changes, believing that it is their right and duty to give leadership and make management decisions. Also, with the increased technological nature of modern industry, many decisions must be made by experts and would not be suitable to be voted on by everyone.

There is also the point, of course, that what works in one country would not necessarily work in another. Yugoslavia's experiments in worker control, for instance, have been made in the context of a Communist government and economy; because of this, they could not easily be imported into Britain. In Britain, unlike Yugoslavia, there are strong, independent trade unions. In practice, British unions have been slightly suspicious of any attempts to introduce industrial democracy which did not involve the union.

When all this is said, it remains true that an enormous amount can be achieved by increasing workers' involvement in what they are doing. An often-quoted example is that of Japan, where in most companies each day starts with a half-hour meeting of managers and workers where suggestions are made and often acted on. In Japan, managers dress no differently from workers and have few special privileges.

Alistair Cooke, the noted broadcaster, mentioned in his radio programme *Letter from America* on 19 February 1982 an unusual development in American industry. A conference of top businessmen had been called. The conference was addressed by a group of Japanese management experts. The Japanese message was "involve your workers, give them increased responsibility and listen to what they have to say". The irony of the situation, Alistair Cooke pointed out, was that Americans, who had taught the world the principles of Scientific Management or Taylorism, were now sitting dutifully at the feet of Oriental businessmen who were preaching almost the exact opposite of those principles.

BOOK LIST

Birch, Lionel (editor), *The History of the TUC 1868-1968. A pictorial survey of a social revolution*, published by the General Council of the TUC

Coates, Ken and Topham, Tony, *Trade Unions in Great Britain*, Spokesman, 1980

Eaton, Jack and Gill, Colin, *The Trade Union Directory – a guide to all trade unions*, Pluto, 1981

Jackson, Michael P., *Trade Unions*, Longman, 1982

Jenkins, David, *Job Power*, Heinemann, 1974

Plant, Martin and Ward, David, *Black Trade Unions in South Africa*, Spokesman, 1982

Smith, C.T.B. and others, *Strikes in Britain*, Manpower paper No. 15, HMSO, 1978

Taylor, John, *Solidarnośé: Five months with Solidarity*, Wildwood House, 1981

Taylor, Robert, *The Fifth Estate. Britain's Unions in the Seventies*, Routledge and Kegan Paul Ltd, 1978

Williamson, Hugh, *The Trade Unions*, Heinemann Educational Ltd, 1981

Films

A selection of films about trade unions available for sale or hire are listed in the Concord films Council catalogue of films.

INDEX